Psychology
in the Talmud

MOSAICA PRESS

שמחת התורה על מסכת ברכות

Psychology
in the Talmud

GUIDELINES FOR **SIMCHAH**
AND **PERSONAL GROWTH**

RABBI ELIHU ABBE, MSW

Published by Mosaica Press, Inc.
www.mosaicapress.com
info@mosaicapress.com

In memory of our parents

LEO T. and BEATRICE ABBE
אליהו טוביה בן קלונימוס ז"ל
פעשא בת זלמן ז"ל

Who helped and inspired the sick
and the needy

Their children
CYRUS AND JUDY ABBE

In honor of our father

HERBERT JAFFE

החבר שמעון בן משה יבל"ח

and in memory of our mother

HENNY JAFFE

רחל בת משה ז"ל

Whose love and devotion to each other
is an inspiration for all of us

Their children
CYRUS AND JUDY ABBE

YOUNG ISRAEL OF RIVERDALE

4502 Henry Hudson Parkway ~ Riverdale, New York 10471

Rabbi Mordechai Willig
718.796.8208

בע"ה

ח' אייר תשע"ב

כא הנכבד

My esteemed talmid Rabbi Elihu Abbe shlita
has written an important and erudite book,
"Simchas Ha Torah," extracting mussar nuggets
from the pages of the Talmud. R' Elihu
himself is a living embodiment of a mussar
personality, as someone who strives for excellence
not only in his Torah scholarship but also in
his fine and refined character. I have
read many pages of the manuscript and have
found this work to be glistening with pearls of
wisdom, and Torah-based insights into the
challenges and potential of the human personality.
I highly recommend this volume.

בברכת התורה וחברה ושא"י,

יונה, ר"ם

TABLE OF CONTENTS

PEREK 1

PEREK 2

PEREK 3

ACKNOWLEDGMENTS

The approach of growth and self-improvement *b'simchah u'v'tuv levav* that is contained in this *sefer* is primarily an outgrowth of absorbing the lessons of life that I have learned in Morasha Kollel. The summers that I have spent in Morasha Kollel have been the most meaningful experiences of my life. *B'nei Torah* in high school, yeshiva, and college, crowned with *ne'imus ha'middos* and a desire to grow in Torah and *kirvas Hashem*, get together for a summer of serious high-level learning, inspiration, comradery, relaxation, and fun in the beautiful outdoors and fresh air of the country. I had the *zechus* to spend two summers as a camper in the High-School Kollel, as well as eleven summers in the College Kollel—six as a camper and five as counselor.

I want to begin by thanking the Rosh Kollel of the High-School Kollel, HaRav Yitzchak Cohen, *shlita*. The inspiration and warmth that he has provided me throughout the years have strengthened me on the path of *ameilus b'Torah* and *avodas Hashem*. He has taught by his own sterling example that it is possible to mix the interpersonal greatness of *chessed l'Avraham*—a soft, warm, and humble personality—together with the *gevurah* of Yitzchak—an unwavering striving for fulfilling the *ratzon Hashem*, into *tiferes l'Yaakov*—a totality of a *talmid chacham* whose *ameilus baTorah* and *hasmadah* is legendary.

There is nobody whom I have learned more from than my Rebbi and Rosh Kollel of the College Kollel, HaGaon HaTzaddik Rav Mordechai Willig, *shlita*. I have gained immensely from Rav Willig's approach of *simchah* and *seichel hayashar* in *avodas Hashem*. Whether it be absorbing Rebbi's *derech halimud* of *l'asukei shemaitsa aliba d'hilchisa*, the inspiration of the *kumzitz*, listening to Rebbi periodically singing out the words of the Gemara during *seder* in a beautiful and powerful voice, watching Rebbi play tennis, observing how pristine logic guides his *hadrachah*, or seeing how much Rebbi does for his *talmidim* as well as for all of Klal Yisrael—there is so much for which I am grateful.

I want to thank my co-counselors in Morasha Kollel, Rabbi Shaya First and Rabbi Dani Yaros, as well as all of the other counselors, for all of the hard work that went into so many amazing summers.

I also want to thank the leadership of Camp Morasha: Jeremy Joszef, Rabbi Aryeh Yudin, and Mr. and Mrs. Spodek, as well as the entire Camp Morasha family. May they merit to continue to inspire the children of Camp Morasha for many years to come.

I want to thank HaGaon HaTzaddik Rav Yona Reiss, *shlita*, for everything that he has done for me. Despite his busy schedule as Menahel of the Yeshiva, and then as Av Beis Din of the Chicago Rabbinical Council, he took out time to give special *shiurim* to me and a group of friends, and then to test and encourage me on my learning. Despite his brilliance and his impressive accomplishments, he is truly one of the most humble people I have ever met. He encourages his *talmidim* and interacts with them as if they were his equals, and this encouragement and appreciation has elevated my spirits on so many occasions. He instilled in me the feeling that I am capable of being successful in my learning and in my ambition to teach Torah. This *sefer* would not have been possible without this *chizuk*, and I am very grateful.

I want to thank my Rosh Yeshiva and Rosh Kollel, HaGaon HaTzaddik Rav Hershel Shachter, *shlita*, for serving as such an outstanding role model in all three pillars on which the world stands. In Torah—just listening to his *shiurim*, expressed with such clarity and quoting so many sources, inspires me to devote even more effort into my learning. In *avodah*—having had the *zechus* to daven at Rav Shachter's minyan for over a decade, I have learned what it means to say each word slowly and with concentration. In *gemilus chassadim*—it is amazing to see how Rav Shachter has time for everyone, never making anyone feel rushed.

I want to thank all of my *rebbeim* at Yeshivas Rabbeinu Yitzchak Elchanan (Yeshiva University) for all the Torah that they have taught me and for the guidance they have provided me: Rabbi Yosef Blau, Rabbi Eliakim Koenigsberg, Rabbi Dovid Miller, Rabbi Yaakov Neuberger, Rabbi Uri Orlian, Rabbi Menachem Penner, Rabbi Eli Baruch Shulman, Rabbi Baruch Simon, Rabbi Zvi Sobolofsky, Rabbi Meir Twersky, and Rabbi Moshe Weinberger.

I want to thank Rabbi Yonason Sacks, Rabbi Yitzchak Genack, Rabbi Shmuel Marcus, and all of the *rebbeim* at Lander College for the wonderful experience that I enjoyed learning in the Lander Beis Medrash during the time that I was living in Queens.

I want to thank Rabbi Ari Jacobson, Dr. Schwalb, and the entire Young Israel of Monsey and Wesley Hills, where I served in my first rabbinic internship. I learned so much from them, and I really appreciate the kindness with which they treated me. They truly left me with such a positive sense of what a community can be.

I want to thank my *rebbeim* at Yeshivat Kerem B'Yavneh: Rabbi Menachem Mendel Blachman, Rabbi Meir Orlian, Rabbi Aharon Silver, Rabbi Shlomo Friedman, and Rabbi Yosef Kritz, as well as my *rebbeim* at MTA, Yeshiva University High School for Boys: Rabbi Shimon Kerner, Rabbi Baruch Pesach Mendelson, Rabbi Gary Beitler, and Rabbi Assaf Bednarsh.

Chazal teach us that we can learn even more from our friends than from our teachers. There are so many friends, *chavrusos*, and role models that I have learned from over the years that it will be impossible to mention all of them. I want to specifically thank: Rabbi Simon Basalely and Rabbi Yakov Grun for being "big brothers" to me for so many years in yeshiva. I also want to specifically thank Rabbi Josh Abramson, Rabbi Daniel Fox, Rabbi Eliron Levinson, Rabbi Aviyam Levinson, Rabbi Menachem Rosenbaum, Rabbi Yaakov Trump, and Dr. Eli Weisenfeld for the friendship, encouragement, and guidance that they have shared with me over the years in yeshiva.

I want to thank *Rabban Shel Yisrael, Mechaneich HaDor*, HaGaon HaTzaddik Rav Yitzchak Zilberstein for the tremendous impact that his *sefarim* have had on my life. His approach of *simchah, gadlus ha'adam, emunah*, and a spiritual and emotional connection to Hakadosh Baruch Hu and Torah that shine from his *sefarim*—*L'Chaneich B'Simchah, Simchah Babayis, Mitzvos B'Simchah, Barchi Nafshi*, and many more—have inspired me and strengthened me and are my regular address whenever I am looking for *chizuk*.

It has been such a pleasure working with Mosaica Press and Rabbi Doron Kornbluth. Rabbi Kornbluth is always easily reachable and very helpful, and he does a wonderful and professional job. The whole process, which was new to me, became a very pleasant and positive experience.

I want to thank my parents, Cyrus and Dr. Judith Abbe, for all of the effort that went into raising me and for everything that they continue to do for my family. I have three children now and I know that raising children is not always easy. Additionally, as it relates to this *sefer*, I want to thank them for teaching us the value of inspiration and personal growth. I remember the stories from Rabbi Paysach Krohn that my father read to me at the Kosel when I was young, and the *divrei Torah* from Rabbi Yissachar Frand that he continues to share at the Shabbos table. Many of the stories and *divrei Torah* revolved around the theme of going the extra mile to do *chessed* for others, a lesson that my father lived by when risking his life to save Jews who were living in oppressive countries. There is always a sense of valuing inspiration and growth. My mother is always an example of care and thoughtfulness for others, both informally and in the way that she uses her medical knowledge to care daily for underprivileged children.

I want to thank my grandparents, Oma and Opa, Herb (*yibadeil l'chaim*) and Henny Jaffe (*a"h*) for everything that they have done for us. My mother learned the *middah* of care and thoughtfulness growing up in their home. It was amazing to watch the love that they always showed each other, and especially the devotion with which Opa cared for Oma while she was ill.

Bubby Pesha passed away when I was very young, and though I remember her and playing at her apartment, it was before I was mature enough to learn from her. I never had the *zechus* to meet Zeidy Elihu Tuvia, and that is why I carry his name. I know that my father's love for inspiration and growth, as well as his drive to push himself to accomplish as much as he can, must have been something that he learned growing up in their home.

I want to thank my siblings, Hava and Dovid Preil, Moshe, and Rivka and Yehoshua Szafransky. They follow in the example set by our parents and grandparents of valuing growth, and showing sensitivity and concern for others.

I want to thank my wife, Eliana, for everything that she does for me and for our children. She does an amazing job caring for three young and active children while preparing lessons and teaching Torah to *talmidos*. It is a pleasure sharing together our goals and dreams of building a beautiful home of *avodas Hashem* with children who will hopefully light up the world with their Torah and mitzvos. Of course, both the writing of this *sefer* and the *limud haTorah* that preceded it would not have been possible without her.

Rochel, Yosef, and Ephraim are such wonderful children. They care for each other and play together so nicely. They love Torah and everything about Yiddishkeit. May they continue to grow in *ahavas haTorah* and *avodas Hashem*!

I want to thank my in-laws, Dr. Harold and Mrs. Sharon Lipsky, for raising such a wonderful daughter and for everything that they continue to do for us and for our children. Recently, I told my two-year-old son and three-year-old daughter, "Do you see that set of *Shas*, all of those Gemaras? Zeidy is a doctor and he helps people feel all better, and he just finished learning all of those Gemaras! And Bubby does so much *chessed* for people in the community and does so many mitzvos!" We are privileged to have parents who set such a good example for our children. I also want to thank my wife's siblings: Rabbi Ari and Michal, Eitan and Tehilla, and Rebecca. It was my friendship with and respect for Eitan before I met Eliana that encouraged me to jump at the opportunity to meet his sister. I will always be grateful for that.

Tov l'hodos la'Shem u'l'zamer l'shimcha elyon! Thank you, Hashem, for enabling me to learn and teach Your precious Torah, and for everything that You do for all of us, *erev, va'voker, v'tzaharayim*. May we merit to thank You *ayin b'ayin b'shuv Hashem Tzion*!

INTRODUCTION

Rav Elazar Menachem Shach, the great Rosh Yeshiva of Ponevezh, once asked his *talmidim*, "How do we know that if a new *talmid* arrives in yeshiva and is sitting alone eating lunch that we should approach him, sit next to him, and make him feel welcome?" The *talmidim* suggested that perhaps the source is the mitzvah to love our fellow man or perhaps the mitzvah to emulate the ways of Hashem. Rav Shach accepted their suggestions but told his *talmidim* that the earliest source is, in fact, from *Parashas Vayeira*. Avraham Avinu, while suffering physical discomfort, invites three angels, who appeared to be idolaters, into his house. He provides them with a delicious meal and serves them personally. He goes out of his way to make them feel at home and comfortable. If under such circumstances, and with such difficulty, Avraham Avinu can go to such lengths for three idolaters, then certainly we can sit down with a new *talmid*, welcome him, and make him feel comfortable.

Rav Shach was teaching his *talmidim* not only about welcoming others and helping them feel comfortable, but also that sections of Torah that are seemingly intended to teach us one primary message may also contain additional important and relevant lessons.

The *Ramban* writes in his famous letter, *Iggeres HaRamban*: "When you conclude a learning session, think about whether there is anything you have learned that you can now implement." Sometimes, we will learn a new halachah that we had not known before. Other times, it will be a new perspective, a new idea, or a new source of inspiration. It may

1

be something that can provide us with guidance, offering either direction or practical advice on how to enhance our lives. When we approach our learning with this goal in mind, we will notice that there are many nuggets of personal growth we might have overlooked if we had not been attuned to them.

Rav Avigdor Miller writes, "The Gemara has a lot of information about how to live a proper life...and you need to assimilate that information...The Gemara is full of wisdom on how to live but you have to learn it...I had a *rebbi, zichrono li'verachah*, who learned in Volozhin, the mother of the yeshivos. When he would say a *shiur* on the Gemara and he would come to something that gave him an excuse to talk about *derech eretz, middos tovos*, and *emunah*, he would always stop and talk about it."[1]

This book focuses on psychological insights from the Talmud, specifically the first three chapters of *Masechta Berachos* (the first tractate of the Talmud). Each idea begins with a quote from the Gemara and a concept of personal growth that we can derive from it. (The quote is translated into English, with background provided in brackets.) The concept is then supported by other statements of Chazal, as well as concepts discussed by secular authors specializing in psychology, personal growth, and inner change. This *sefer* is intended to serve as an example of how much we can learn about change, growth—and ourselves—when we are attuned to deriving lessons from the holy words of the Tanna'im and Amora'im.

The Mishnah in *Avos* teaches us that all wisdom is contained in the Torah.[2] The *Ramban* in his introduction to his commentary on Chumash elaborates on this concept. He quotes the Gemara that states that Hashem created fifty categories of wisdom and understanding in the world.[3] These include the categories of inanimate stone, of vegetation, of trees, of living animals, of birds, of fish, of mankind, of the soul, of the heavenly beings, etc. Moshe Rabbeinu was taught all of the wisdom

---

1   *Rabbi Avigdor Miller Speaks*, p. 73.

2   *Avos* 5:22.

3   *Rosh Hashanah* 21b.

pertaining to forty-nine of the fifty categories. Only the category of knowledge of Hashem's essence was hidden from him—and from mankind. The *Ramban* tells us that all of this wisdom that was taught to Moshe was written in the Torah, either explicitly or through hints.

Why, then, quote secular authors? While all wisdom is contained in the Torah, it is frequently difficult to uncover the wisdom when you do not know what you are seeking. After seeing an idea discussed in a book of personal growth, it is easier to notice when Chazal convey a similar message. The Gemara in *Bava Metzia* tells us that Rabbi Yochanan taught a particular halachah. He was then questioned that since the halachah that he taught is evident from a careful reading of the Mishnah, why was it necessary for him to repeat it? Rabbi Yochanan responded, "Had I not lifted the shard, you would not have found the pearl underneath it,"[4]—i.e., if I had not taught the halachah and called attention to it, it would have been difficult to notice that the halachah is in fact contained within the Mishnah. Similarly, at times, if not for having seen a concept in a personal growth book, we would not have discovered the pearl contained in the words of Chazal.

May we enjoy learning and growing together as we internalize the messages of growth that shine from the holy words of Chazal!

---

4   *Bava Metzia* 17b.

PEREK 1

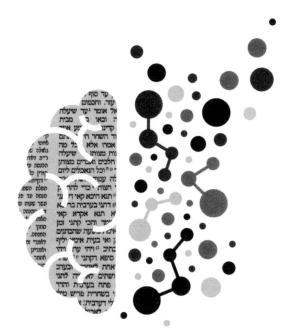

2a

SEE THE WORLD THROUGH POSITIVE CORE BELIEFS

מאי שנא דתני בערבית ברישא? לתני דשחרית
ברישא!

[The *masechta* begins with discussing the time for saying the evening *Shema*. The Gemara questions:] Why is the evening *Shema* taught first? The morning *Shema* should have been taught first.

The halachic day begins at night. *Tosafos* therefore questions why the Gemara would suggest that the Mishnah begin with a discussion of the morning *Shema*. *Tosafos* answers that when the Torah discusses the *Korban Tamid* (daily sacrifice), the morning offering is mentioned first. This could serve as a precedent for discussing the morning *Shema* before the evening *Shema*.

Another answer is offered by the *Shitah Mekubetzes*. David HaMelech, in *Tehillim*, exclaims: "The introduction of Your words illuminates, making simpletons understand."[1] The *Shitah Mekubetzes* learns from this verse that the introduction to one's words should be filled with light. The

---

1 *Tehillim* 119:130.

morning is a time of light, and therefore the discussion of the morning *Shema* should precede the discussion of the evening *Shema*. (The Gemara proceeds to explain why in this case the Mishnah began by discussing the evening *Shema* first, notwithstanding this important principle.)

The Gemara in *Bava Basra* teaches us that when Chazal sought to organize halachos, they generally followed a principle that אתחולי בפורענותא לא מתחלינן, "One does not begin with catastrophe."[2] Halachos pertaining to very unfortunate situations are to be taught last.

When someone begins their words with positivity, it indicates that their focus is on the positive. When you see the world as a positive and cheerful place, this perspective will be evident in your speech.

The foundation of Cognitive Behavioral Therapy (CBT) is the idea that events don't lead directly to emotions. It is our thoughts and perceptions about the event that lead to the emotion. Sometimes, these thoughts are conscious, and we recognize having them. At other times, they are subtle (even automatic) thoughts that would go unnoticed if we weren't looking for them.

Every person has certain core beliefs about themselves, other people, and the world. These core beliefs affect the automatic thoughts that a person will have in any given situation. Two people can have very different emotional reactions to the same event, stemming from their different core beliefs.

From the Gemara's question as to why the Mishnah didn't begin with the logical choice of morning before evening, Chazal are teaching us, on the very first page of the Talmud, that we are to work on ourselves to develop positive core beliefs. When we view the world as a place of light and happiness, our focus will be on the positive. This attitude will be evident in our speech. We will begin our conversations with positivity and light and infuse happiness into all of those around us as well.

Develop positive core beliefs and your focus, speech, and self-talk will gravitate to the positive.

---

2   *Bava Basra* 108a.

2b

APPRECIATE HASHEM'S GIFTS IN NATURE

מאימתי קורין את שמע בערבין? משהעני נכנס
לאכול פתו במלח.

[The Gemara quotes a *Beraisa* that states:] From when
can one recite the evening *Shema*? From when a poor
person enters to eat his bread dipped in salt.

Rashi explains that a poor person begins his dinner early because he cannot afford a candle.

Light is a necessity, and during daylight hours it is available in abundance for everyone, regardless of how poor they may be. The sun is a source of light, happiness, and energy that Hakadosh Baruch Hu provides for each person, every day.

The *Chovos Halevavos* notes that one of the favors that Hashem does for us is creating larger quantities of that which is more essential and lesser quantities of what is less essential. Nobody can survive without air, and it is therefore found everywhere. Water is also essential and is plentiful, but since we can survive without it for a longer period of time, it is less plentiful than air. Food is a necessity and bountiful, although less available than water. Objects that do not have inherent value, such as gold or jewels, are much more rare.[1] In other words, Hashem, in his kindness, sees to it that we have everything that we need. Sunlight is another wonderful example of this concept. It is a necessity for everyone, and therefore it is plentiful. A poor man who can't afford candles can benefit from this kindness of Hashem.

Rav Avigdor Miller makes numerous observations about the *berachah* of sunlight. He writes:

> *The food cycle begins with plant life, and all plants require light to create their own food through photosynthesis...The sun provides the energy that makes everything work on this earth...When you study the sunlight, you see how it cooperates with this earth in so many ways that it involves the most cunning planning, blueprints of scheming that needed an intelligence far beyond that of any human being. The purpose of light is to let you know, "Baruch Atah Hashem, Yotzeir hame'oros."*[2]

Light is only one example of the many things that we benefit from constantly that we sometimes overlook. If we don't notice the favor that Hashem gives us, we miss out on deriving the full pleasure from it. The *Chovos Halevavos* writes:

> *It is the responsibility of Torah scholars in each generation to inspire those who don't recognize Hashem's kindness and to teach them the wonderful benefits. There is so much goodness that recipients do not enjoy because they don't recognize the gift or appreciate its value. When you inspire the recipients to recognize the value of these gifts, they praise and thank Hashem. They enjoy the pleasures in this world and receive reward in the next world as well.*[3]

Appreciate all of the goodness that Hashem bestows on us.
Even the basic elements of nature can be enjoyed.

---

1   *Chovos Halevavos, Shaar Habechinah*, chap. 5.
2   *Rabbi Avigdor Miller Speaks*, vol. 2, p. 92.
3   *Chovos Halevavos, Shaar Habechinah*, introduction.

3a

EFFECTIVE COMMUNICATION

מאי קסבר רבי אליעזר? אי קסבר שלש משמרות
הוי הלילה—לימא עד ארבע שעות! ואי קסבר ארבע
משמרות הוי הלילה—לימא עד שלש שעות!

[Rabbi Eliezer had taught in the Mishnah that one may
recite the evening *Shema* until the end of the first watch
of the night (of angels who offer heavenly song). The
Gemara questions:] What does Rabbi Eliezer believe? If
he believes that there are three watches over the course
of the night, he should have said, "Until the end of the
fourth hour" [for the night consists of twelve halachic
hours]. If he believes that there are four watches over
the course of the night, he should have said, "Until the
end of the third hour."

Rashi explains that Rabbi Eliezer should have mentioned a recognizable time, rather than saying, "the end of the third watch." While it
may have been clear to Rabbi Eliezer himself what his intentions were,
it may not be clear to the listener. (The Gemara goes on to explain why

"the end of third watch" is, in fact, a recognizable time that the listener would understand.)

The Gemara in *Pesachim* states that a person does not know what his friend is thinking.[1] All too often there are misunderstandings simply because of a miscommunication. It is the responsibility of the speaker to make sure that what is clear to him can also be understood clearly by the listener. This is both in terms of the clarity of the message and the perspective behind the message.

Before a rabbi is authorized to issue a halachic ruling, he must receive *semichah*. The Gemara questions, "If he has learned [and knows the answer to the halachic question], why must he have *semichah* to issue a ruling?" The Gemara answers by relating a story of a student who once issued a ruling that was misunderstood because two Hebrew words sound almost identical. The entire town adopted a mistaken practice as a result. It was at that time that Chazal decreed that a student may not issue a ruling without obtaining permission from his *rebbi* (i.e., *semichah*), who would ensure that he would speak clearly when issuing rulings.[2]

Effective communication is not limited to speaking in a way that the other person will understand. It also requires understanding the other's perspective and tailoring the message to fit their understanding and viewpoint.

At the beginning of *Parashas Pinchas*, the Torah tells us that Pinchas was the son of Elazar, the son of Aharon HaKohen. *Rashi* explains that people mocked Pinchas. How could the descendent of an idol worshipper (Pinchas descended from Yisro) have the audacity to kill Zimri, the leader of *Shevet* Shimon? The Torah therefore tells us that Pinchas was also the son and grandson of very important people—Elazar and Aharon, respectively.

This *Rashi* is troubling. Pinchas did what was right. He witnessed a crime in which the halachah calls for action. The Torah should have responded to the mockers that it doesn't matter who one's ancestors

---

1   *Pesachim* 54b.
2   *Sanhedrin* 5b.

are when it comes to doing what's right. Why did the Torah validate the perspective of those who inappropriately mocked Pinchas?

We see from here the importance of communicating within the framework of the other person's understanding. Hashem told the mockers that even having accepted their underlying rule that one who has limited ancestry must not combat one who has dignified ancestry, it was still appropriate for Pinchas to act.

The same idea can be seen when Hashem sends Moshe to Mitzrayim. Moshe is hesitant to accept the mission because he has difficulty speaking, and he does not want to hurt Aharon's feelings. Until then, Aharon had led the people, and so now Moshe doesn't want to usurp his leadership. Hashem validates both of these concerns. He tells Moshe that just as He gives speech to the mute, so too, he will help Moshe overcome his difficulty speaking. He also validates Moshe's concern for Aharon by telling him that he need not worry, because Aharon is truly happy at heart to see Moshe lead the people.

Why is this necessary? Moshe should simply be told, "I'm G-d and I'm telling you to go to Mitzrayim. Please don't ask Me any questions." Instead, Hashem teaches us to put ourselves in the other person's shoes, understand the situation from their perspective, and address each of their concerns.

Effective communication requires understanding where the listener is coming from, addressing their perspective, and speaking in a clear and understandable manner.

3b

SOCIAL COMFORT

אין אומרין בפני המת אלא דבריו של מת. אמר רבי
אבא בר כהנא: לא אמרן אלא בדברי תורה, אבל
מילי דעלמא לית לן בה.

One may not discuss anything in front of the deceased
other than relating words of the deceased himself.
Said Rabbi Abba bar Kahana, "This is only with regard
to words of Torah. When it comes to worldly matters,
anything may be discussed."

Rashi explains that it is forbidden to discuss Torah in front of the deceased because the soul of the deceased is pained that he is unable to participate. It is permitted to have mundane conversations because there is nothing negative about remaining silent from a mundane conversation.

The CBT model of social phobia consists of three steps: anticipatory processing, heightened self-consciousness, and post-processing:

- Anticipatory processing is the fear of the upcoming social event. The person may worry and prepare excessively.
- The second step is heightened self-consciousness during the event itself. The person directs his focus on himself in a

14

judgmental manner, assuming that his anxiety is very no-
ticeable and that he is not interacting optimally. This focus
prevents him from being present in the situation and leads to
an anxiety-induced skill deficit. The person doesn't perform
optimally because of his anxiety, which in turn confirms his fear
of social ineptitude. This strengthens his belief and leads to the
recurrence of the fear in the future.

- The final step is post-event rumination, where the person re-
views the interaction in his mind with excessive focus on the
negative aspects of the interaction. Because of his beliefs about
himself, he is very attuned to any information that will confirm
his belief. This is known as confirmation bias. Any negative
aspect of the interaction looms large, whereas any evidence of
social success is unnoticed or discounted.

A common theme present in social phobia is the fear of "I won't know
what to say. I'll be silent. People will think that I'm awkward." This
theme is present during anticipatory processing and then again in the
heightened self-consciousness during the event.

Our *Rashi* can help alleviate this aspect of the anxiety. We are not
to be judgmental of our abilities to involve ourselves in conversations.
There is nothing negative about remaining quiet. In fact, the Mishnah
at the end of the first chapter of *Pirkei Avos* teaches us that silence is a
laudatory trait. This perspective enables a person to feel more comfortable and ultimately leads to their increased social involvement.

Even for those who don't experience social phobia, the same three steps
can occur when one is anxious about speaking publicly, an upcoming social
event, or an upcoming conversation with a boss or a difficult individual.
By recognizing that some of our anxiety is founded on a fear of not living
up to social expectations—which are not inherently valuable—we can
minimize the anxiety and be more successful in the interaction.

Overcome social anxiety with the following three steps: Don't be afraid
of falling short of social expectations, focus on the interaction and not
on yourself, and don't judge your social performance negatively.

3b

WHAT, HOW, AND WHY?

ושואלין באורים ותומים.

[In the times of David HaMelech, there was a procedure that would precede going out to battle. One of the steps of this procedure was inquiring from the *Urim V'Tumim*. The *Urim V'Tumim* was a written name of Hashem that was placed in the *Choshen* (breastplate) and worn by the Kohen Gadol. It was through this name of Hashem that the Hebrew letters written on the *Choshen* would light up in response to questions posed.]

And they would ask of the *Urim V'Tumim*.

Rashi comments that they would ask the *Urim V'Tumim* if they would be successful in battle. Seemingly, this is obvious. If the Gemara tells us that before going to battle they would inquire of the *Urim V'Tumim*, obviously they were inquiring about whether or not they would be successful. What is *Rashi* trying to teach us?

At the end of *Sefer Shoftim*, we learn about an unfortunate civil war between *Shevet* Binyamin and the rest of the Jewish People. Before going to war, the Jewish People ask Hashem "Which *shevet* should commence the battle?" Hashem responds "*Shevet* Yehudah." Yehudah leads the people

16

into battle, and they are soundly defeated by *Shevet* Binyamin. They return and cry before Hashem and ask if they should continue fighting. Hashem replies that indeed they should. Again, they go to battle and again they are soundly defeated. They cry, fast, and bring offerings to Hashem. Again, they ask if they should continue to fight, and this time Hashem says, "Go up and fight, because tomorrow I will give them over into your hands." Indeed, this third time they were successful in battle. *Rashi* comments that the first two times the Jewish People did not inquire if they would be successful. Only by the last time did they ask if they would win the battle, and that is when Hashem told them that indeed they would.[1] (The *Malbim* explains that it was only before the third battle that the Jewish People repentended completely from their sins.)

Perhaps this is what our *Rashi* is trying to teach us: It is not sufficient to know only if what we are doing is right. We must also know if we are doing it in a way that will be effective. They were not only meant to ask the *Urim V'Tumim* if they should go to battle, but also if they would succeed. Had they asked, they would have learned that they would not be successful. Perhaps they would then have engaged in introspection and repentance and thus merited success in the first battle.

In describing what it takes to form good habits, Stephen Covey writes, "For our purposes, we will define habit as the intersection of knowledge, skill and desire. Knowledge is the theoretical paradigm, the what to do and the why. Skill is the how to do it. And desire is the motivation, the want to do. In order to make something happen in our lives, we have to have all three."[2] Motivation, desire, and the knowledge of why something is important must be coupled with the understanding of what to do and the skill necessary to do it.

The recipe for success: Motivation, the knowledge of what to do, and the skill of how to do it. All three areas are arenas for growth and enhance success.

---

1   *Shoftim* 20:18.
2   Stephen Covey, *The Seven Habits of Highly Effective People*, p. 55.

4a

HASHEM'S CHILDREN

ראוים היו ישראל ליעשות להם נס בימי עזרא כדרך
שנעשה להם בימי יהושע בן נון, אלא שגרם החטא.

When the Jewish People returned from exile with
Ezra, they were worthy of miracles—the likes of which
Hashem had performed in the times of the original
entry into Eretz Yisrael under Yehoshua. Unfortunately,
sin prevented this from becoming a reality.

If sin caused the Jewish People to no longer merit a miracle, then why
does the Gemara say that they were worthy of a miracle? Seemingly,
the Gemara should have taught instead, "The Jewish People would have
been worthy of a miracle if not for them having sinned."

We learn from here that the Jewish People are inherently worthy of
miracles even when they sin. The concept of reward and punishment
demands that sins be punished and that the miracle not be performed,
but the inherent elevated level of the Jewish People remains intact.

When the Jewish People entered Eretz Yisrael, they were commanded
not to take from the spoils of Yericho. Achan violated the command,
and Hashem punished the people with the death of thirty-six Jewish
soldiers in the next battle that they fought at Ai. Yehoshua and the

elders mourned and davened fervently. Hashem came to Yehoshua and replied, "The Jewish People (*Yisrael*) have sinned." The Gemara notes that despite the tragic sin resulting in so many deaths, they are still referred to as "The Jewish People (Yisrael)."[1] *Rashi* explains that this is because this name "Yisrael" indicates the holiness of the people, and it remains intact even after sinning.

The Gemara in *Kiddushin* quotes the opinion of Rabbi Meir, who notes that even when the Jewish People were sinning greatly, they were still called Hashem's children.[2] In the haftarah that we read before Tishah B'Av, the Navi Yeshayahu severely admonishes the people for their many sins. He refers to the people as "destructive children." Rabbi Meir highlights that even when the Jewish People sin greatly, they are still referred to as Hashem's children.

This is an important recognition on both the communal level, affecting our perspectives on the Jewish People as a whole, as well as on a personal level. Nobody is perfect. Sometimes we fail to live up to the high standards that we set for ourselves. Sometimes we even sin. Nonetheless, our *neshamos* remain pure. We do not fall from our inherently elevated status of being Hashem's children.

Our essence remains elevated and pure even when we sin, both on a personal level and on a communal level.

1   *Sanhedrin* 44a.
2   *Kiddushin* 36a.

4b

PLANNING OUR GROWTH
CAREFULLY

חכמים עשו סייג לדבריהם, כדי שלא יהא אדם בא
מן השדה בערב ואומר: אלך לביתי ואוכל קימעא
ואשתה קימעא ואישן קימעא, ואחר כך אקרא
קריאת שמע ואתפלל. וחוטפתו שינה ונמצא ישן
כל הלילה; אבל אדם בא מן השדה בערב, נכנס
לבית הכנסת, אם רגיל לקרות קורא, ואם רגיל
לשנות שונה, וקורא קריאת שמע ומתפלל, ואוכל
פתו ומברך.

[The *Chachamim* rule that one must say *Shema* before midnight. Technically, they agree with Rabban Gamliel that one may say the *Shema* until dawn. However, they required saying *Shema* before midnight due to the following concern:] The *Chachamim* established a protective fence so that a person not return from the field in the evening and say, "I will go home and eat a little, drink a little, and sleep a little, and then I will say *Shema* and daven." Ultimately, he will be overcome by sleep and sleep the entire night [without saying *Shema*]. Rather, a

person should return from the field in the evening and
enter the shul. If he is accustomed to learning Chumash,
he learns Chumash; if he is accustomed to learning
Mishnah, he learns Mishnah. Then he recites *Shema* and
davens, eats his bread, and says *Birkas Hamazon*.

One of the components of Cognitive Behavioral Therapy (CBT) for
depression is behavioral activation. When someone is depressed, they
tend to recoil to themselves and cease from involvement in activities
that could give them pleasure or a sense of mastery. They tell themselves
that they don't have the energy to be active. They find themselves in a
vicious cycle where depression saps the energy they need to be active,
which in turn takes away opportunities for pleasure and a sense of
mastery, which results in worsening depression. Behavioral activation
refers to intentionally scheduling activities that can provide pleasure
or a sense of mastery. It is necessary to devote considerable thought
to scheduling activities. If the schedule is not very specific, it likely will
not be carried out. It is also necessary to consider all of the possible
thoughts that may arise and discourage the individual from performing
the activity. These thoughts can then be addressed and countered.

Chazal knew that while it is easy to say that *Shema* must be recited
before dawn, after a long day's work in the field, it is probable that
thoughts will arise and impede the likelihood that the requirement will
be fulfilled. They anticipated a person telling himself, "I will go home, I
will eat a bit, have something to drink, and then I will say *Shema*." It is
quite possible that they will then sleep until morning. Seeing this very
human problem, Chazal delineated a very specific plan for a person to
go straight from the field to the shul, learn a little, say *Shema*, and then
go home for dinner and bed.

The *Mesilas Yesharim* writes in his introduction:

> *Piety, fear of Heaven, love, and purity of heart are not natural
> emotions to a person such that they wouldn't require effort to*

acquire them...They require means and strategies to acquire
them. There is no shortage of impediments that distance them,
and there is no lack of methods for distancing the impediments.
It is therefore necessary to invest time to this study to recog-
nize the truths of the matter and to know the way to acquire
and fulfill them.

In areas in which we hope to grow, we need more than just positive goals. We need to give forethought to what might stand in the way and what we can do specifically to overcome those impediments. We have to think about what thoughts may interfere with our growth as well as what external impediments may arise. When we devote the time to this analysis, we will see great success.

Plan your growth. Anticipate obstacles and plan how you
will overcome them.

5a

CONSTRUCTIVE DISCOMFORT

שלש מתנות טובות נתן הקדוש ברוך הוא לישראל,
וכולן לא נתנן אלא על ידי יסורין. אלו הן: תורה וארץ
ישראל והעולם הבא.

Hashem gave three good gifts to the Jewish People,
and all of them were given through suffering. They are:
Torah, Eretz Yisrael, and the World to Come.

When thinking about our goals, Robert Leahy writes that we have
to ask ourselves not only "What is my goal?" but also "What do I have to
do to get it?" and "Am I willing to do it?" He continues,

> *If you plan to solve some of your problems, you may have to
> do some things that you find uncomfortable...In order to do
> things that you do not want to do, you will need to change your
> attitude toward discomfort by making discomfort your goal.
> You will not make any real progress unless you are uncomfort-
> able. If you procrastinate, then you are a "discomfort dodger,"
> constantly avoiding things that make you uncomfortable.*[1]

---

1   Robert Leahy, *The Worry Cure*, p. 90.

Leahy calls this concept "constructive discomfort." It is a necessary step of personal growth and reminds us of the Mishnah in *Pirkei Avos* that states: "The reward is commensurate with the effort."[2] *Rashi* explains that this Mishnah was taught in Aramaic rather than Hebrew because it was a common expression, and the Mishnah wanted to relate it in the language in which it was usually said. While of course it is true on a metaphysical level in terms of Hashem's heavenly reward, it was also a common expression codified by the Mishnah in terms of practical worldly success as well.

Rabbi Yehudah HaNasi taught: "Calculate the [small and immediate] loss incurred in performing a mitzvah in comparison with its [great and eternal] reward. Calculate the [small and immediate] benefit of sin in comparison with its [severe and eternal] loss."[3] We are not blind to the discomfort that doing good sometimes entails. We just know that it is worthwhile!

The Gemara in *Nedarim* relates that when Rabbi Yehudah would go to the *beis midrash* to study, he would carry with him a large pitcher that could be used as a chair. He exclaimed, "Great is work, for it brings honor to the one who does it."[4] The *Ran* explains that since he carried a chair with him, he would not need to sit on the floor. Even though carrying the chair was not easy (it was "work"), it was worthwhile to invest the effort.

Leahy recommends that we create a list of all of the uncomfortable things that we have successfully done in the past and how productive they were. This can motivate us to put in that extra effort.

Constructive discomfort is necessary for success and growth.
Assess how it has helped you in the past and determine to embrace
it in the future.

---

2   *Avos* 5:23.
3   Ibid., 2:1.
4   *Nedarim* 49b.

5b

A RELAXED APPROACH TO MINOR INCONVENIENCES

אמר רבי יוחנן: נגעים...אינן יסורין של אהבה. ונגעים
לא? והתניא: כל מי שיש בו אחד מארבעה מראות
נגעים הללו—אינן אלא מזבח כפרה!—מזבח כפרה
הוו, יסורין של אהבה לא הוו. ואי בעית אימא: הא
לן והא להו.

Rabbi Yochanan says, "Contracting *tzaraas*...is not a
form of 'afflictions of love.'" Is this really true? Have we
not learned in a *Beraisa* that the four types of *tzaraas*
are an altar of atonement? They are an atonement, but
they are not "afflictions of love."

Alternatively, the difference is whether it is for us [who
live in Bavel] or for them [who live in Eretz Yisrael].

Rashi explains that contracting *tzaraas* always serves as an atonement for one's sins. In Eretz Yisrael, one who contracts *tzaraas* would be
obligated to leave the city. This was a significant burden. It is therefore
not a sign of "afflictions of love," the suffering that Hashem bestows
on the righteous as a means of increasing their reward in the world to

come. In Bavel, the *metzora* was not obligated to leave the city. Because contracting *tzaraas* was therefore only a minor inconvenience, it was a sign of "afflictions of love."

The Gemara in *Avodah Zarah* quotes a pasuk in *Amos* that reads, "Only you have I known from among all the families of the earth; therefore, I will hold you responsible for all your sins."[1] The Gemara questions: "Does one who has anger direct it at the one who he loves?" Why does the *pasuk* say that it is specifically because Hashem knows and loves us that He holds us accountable for our sins? The Gemara answers with a parable of a lender who is owed money by two different borrowers. From the borrower who he dislikes, he insists that he be repaid in full immediately. From the borrower who he loves, he collects the payment over time in small increments.[2] So too, because of Hashem's love for us, He allows us to "pay" for our sins in small increments with (only) minor inconveniences. This saves us from more significant punishment that would be more difficult to tolerate.

Richard Carlson, in the introduction to his book, *Don't Sweat the Small Stuff, and It's All Small Stuff*, discusses the importance of having a healthy approach to minor inconveniences. He writes:

> When we are immobilized by little things—when we are irritated, annoyed, and easily bothered—our overreactions not only make us frustrated but actually get in the way of getting what we want. We lose sight of the bigger picture, focus on the negative, and annoy other people who might otherwise help us. In short, we live our lives as if they were one great big emergency! We often rush around looking busy, trying to solve problems, but in reality, we are often compounding them. Because everything seems like such a big deal, we end up spending our lives dealing with one drama after another...Happily, there is another way to relate to life—a softer, more graceful path that makes life seem easier and the people in it more compatible.

---

1   *Amos* 3:2.
2   *Avodah Zarah* 4a.

This "other way" of living involves replacing old habits of "reaction" with new habits of perspective. These new habits enable us to have richer, more satisfying lives.

Don't be overwhelmed by minor inconveniences. Accept them as a part of life and even appreciate them for their positive spiritual benefit.

5b

FOCUS ON YOUR CIRCLE
OF INFLUENCE

רבי אלעזר חלש, על לגביה רבי יוחנן. חזא דהוה
קא גני בבית אפל, גלייה לדרעיה ונפל נהורא. חזייה
דהוה קא בכי רבי אלעזר. אמר ליה: אמאי קא
בכית? אי משום תורה דלא אפשת—שנינו: אחד
המרבה ואחד הממעיט ובלבד שיכוין לבו לשמים!
ואי משום מזוני—לא כל אדם זוכה לשתי שלחנות!
ואי משום בני—דין גרמא דעשיראה ביר. אמר ליה:
להאי שופרא דבלי בעפרא קא בכינא. אמר ליה: על
דא ודאי קא בכית, ובכו תרוייהו.

Rabbi Elazar became ill. Rabbi Yochanan went to visit
him. When he saw that he was sleeping in a dark home,
he revealed his arm and cast light in the room. Noticing
that Rabbi Elazar was crying, he asked him, "Why do you
cry? If it is because of the Torah knowledge that you
have not attained, we have learned that one who does
more and one who does less are equivalent, provided
that their intentions are for the sake of Heaven. If it
is that you are not wealthy enough to buy ample food,

not everyone merits having wealth in both this world and the next. And if it is because you have lost children, this is the bone of my tenth son (Rabbi Yochanan lost all ten of his sons). Rabbi Elazar answered, "I cry because this beautiful one is enveloped in dust. Rabbi Yochanan replied, "For this you certainly cry," and the two of them cried together.

Why was Rabbi Elazar crying? How are we to understand his response that he is crying because of "this beautiful one who is enveloped in dust?"

The *Maharsha* quotes a Gemara in *Bava Metzia* where Rabbi Yochanan says that he is a remnant of the beautiful inhabitants of Yerushalayim from before the destruction of the Beis Hamikdash.[1] He explains that Rabbi Elazar was crying over the realization that when Rabbi Yochanan would pass away, there would no longer be anything left from the glory and beauty of the Beis Hamikdash era of Yerushalayim. In effect, Rabbi Elazar was mourning the destruction of the Beis Hamikdash.

Why do we mourn the destruction of the Beis Hamikdash? Is it not crying over the past? What will our tears accomplish?

The Gemara in *Bava Basra* tells us that anyone who mourns over the destruction of Yerushalayim will merit to see its time of joy when it is rebuilt.[2] Rav Pincus explains that in any loving relationship the love is strengthened when each person sees that the other truly cares about them.[3] Our way of demonstrating to Hashem that we truly care about Him is by mourning the loss of the close relationship that we had when the Beis Hamikdash stood. When we show Hashem how much we care about Him, our relationship is strengthened and we will merit to see the joy of Yerushalayim.

---

1   *Bava Metzia* 84a.
2   *Bava Basra* 60b.
3   Rav Shimshon Pincus, *Nefesh Shimshon: Galus V'Nechamah*, p. 141.

When Rabbi Yochanan heard that this was the cause of Rabbi Elazar's tears, he acknowledged that this was certainly a reason to cry, and he began to cry as well.

In addition to the obvious significance of tears over the destruction of the Beis Hamikdash, perhaps there is another lesson that we can learn from the Gemara's story. Rabbi Yochanan originally thought that Rabbi Elazer was crying because he had not learned as much Torah as he would have liked, or was not as wealthy as he would have liked to be. If Rabbi Elazar was crying over Torah, Rabbi Yochanan comforted him by saying that as long as one has studied Torah to the best of their ability, with the right intentions, they are no less than someone who has studied more. Not everyone has the same abilities and a person is only asked to live up to their own potential. If Rabbi Elazar was crying over wealth, Rabbi Yochanan told him that not everyone is fortunate enough to be wealthy. In essence, Rabbi Yochanan was telling Rabbi Elazar not to cry over something that he couldn't attain.

Scholarship of the highest level and wealth may have been outside of Rabbi Elazar's ability. It did, however, make sense for Rabbi Elazar to cry over something within his control. Mourning over Yerushalayim demonstrates a personal connection to Hashem. It merits the individual with ultimately seeing the joy of Yerushalayim. The tears shed are not useless. The crying is constructive.

Stephen Covey writes:

> *Proactive people focus their efforts in the Circle of Influence. They work on the things they can do something about. The nature of their energy is positive, enlarging, and magnifying, causing their Circle of Influence to increase. Reactive People, on the other hand, focus their efforts in the Circle of Concern. They focus on the weaknesses of other people, the problems in the environment, and circumstances over which they have no control. Their focus results in blaming and accusing attitudes, reactive language, and increased feelings of victimization. The negative energy generated by that focus, combined with*

neglect in areas they could do something about, causes their Circle of Influence to shrink.[4]

Focus your attention on areas where you can be constructive.

---

4   *Seven Habits*, p. 90.

5b

SETTING ACCOMPLISHABLE GOALS

אמר להו: קבילנא עלי דיהיבנא ליה. איכא דאמרי:
הדר חלא והוה חמרא; ואיכא דאמרי: אייקר חלא
ואיזדבן בדמי דחמרא.

[Rav Huna had four hundred barrels of wine that spoiled and became vinegar. The rabbis went to visit him and instructed him to do a personal accounting of his actions to determine if he had sinned. When he asked if they suspected him of doing something wrong, they replied that if Hashem punished him, He surely had a just reason. They then informed him that they were aware that he had denied his sharecropper his fair share of the vines. Even though the sharecropper had stolen other things from Rav Huna, this was not a reason to withhold the vines that did rightfully belong to the sharecropper.] Rav Huna said, "I accept upon myself to give them to him." Some say that the vinegar miraculously became wine. Others say that the value of vinegar increased and it was sold for the same price as wine.

As soon as Rav Huna agreed to give his sharecropper his portion of the vines, the vinegar miraculously became wine.

Rabbeinu Yonah writes, in *Shaarei Teshuvah*, that as soon as a person accepts upon himself to do as he is instructed by the *chachmei haTorah*, it is considered as if he has already fulfilled the mitzvos that he will ultimately fulfill as a result.[1] Similarly, if a person intends to perform a mitzvah and then extenuating circumstances prevent him from doing so, he is nonetheless credited as if he has performed the mitzvah.[2]

The Gemara in *Nedarim* quotes a dispute between Rabbi Meir and Rabbi Yehudah.[3] Rabbi Meir is of the opinion that it is better not to take an oath than to take an oath and fulfill it. This is because the likelihood is great that one will end up forgetting to fulfill it. Rabbi Yehudah argues and says that if one will fulfill their oath, it is best to take it. The *pasuk* says, "It is better not to take an oath than to take one and not fulfill it." The implication is that the best option is to take an oath and make sure to fulfill it.

The *Ran* questions that, seemingly, the *pasuk* is obvious. Certainly, it is better not to take an oath at all than to take an oath and not fulfill it. Why is this *pasuk* necessary?

He answers that one might have thought that one receives a reward for his devotion at the time one takes an oath. If later he forgets to fulfill it or something beyond his control prevents him from fulfilling it, one might think that he doesn't lose out on the reward that he has already earned. The *pasuk* therefore tells us that one only receives reward at the time the oath is fulfilled, and not at the time it is taken.

How are we to understand this idea of the *Ran* in light of the Rabbeinu Yonah and the Gemara in *Berachos* (6a) that teach that as soon as one decides to fulfill a mitzvah, it is considered as if he has already fulfilled it, and that he receives reward even if something beyond his control prevents him from ultimately performing the mitzvah?

---

1   *Shaarei Teshuvah* 2:10.
2   *Berachos* 6a.
3   *Nedarim* 9a.

Presumably the answer to this question is that there is a difference between oaths and mitzvos: One gets credit for a mitzvah as soon as one intends to perform it, while one only gets credit for an oath at the time that he actually fulfills it. What is the reason for this distinction?

Oaths were frequently taken either in situations of distress or in gratitude after experiencing something wonderful. In these situations, a person would accept upon himself commitments of a magnitude that he would not have accepted in a normal situation. Unfortunately, these types of resolutions are all too often not kept. Mitzvos, on the other hand, are of a more basic and common nature, and the person has usually fulfilled them many times in the past. This type of commitment will much more likely be fulfilled. When one commits to do something that they will, in all likelihood, fulfill, they get credit as soon as they accept it upon themselves.

There is an important lesson that we can learn from here about setting goals. Commitments that we make must be small and accomplishable so that we can grow realistically, one step at a time.

John Maxwell writes:

> *When you attempt too much too soon, you're almost guaranteed to fall short of your desired results. That is demotivating. The secret to building motivational momentum is to start small with the simple stuff. Begin by setting goals that are worthwhile but highly achievable. Master the basics. Then practice them every day without fail. Small disciplines repeated with consistency every day lead to great achievements gained slowly over time. If you want to grow, don't try to win big. Try to win small.*[4]

Set small goals that you can accomplish. This will motivate you to continue growing.

---

4   John Maxwell, *How Successful People Grow*, p. 41.

5b-6a

THE BEAUTY OF HUMILITY

תניא, אבא בנימין אומר: שנים שנכנסו להתפלל,
וקדם אחד מהם להתפלל ולא המתין את חברו
ויצא...ואם המתין לו מה שכרו? אמר רבי יוסי ברבי
חנינא: זוכה לברכות הללו, שנאמר: לוא הקשבת
למצותי ויהי כנהר שלומך וצדקתך כגלי הים ויהי
כחול זרעך וצאצאי מעיך וגו'.

Abba Binyamin says, "Two people who enter [a shul] to
daven, and one finishes davening first and leaves without waiting for his friend..." And if he waits for him, what
is his reward? Rabbi Yosi ben Rabbi Chaninah says, "He
merits the *berachos* of the following *pasuk*, 'Because
you listened to my mitzvos [*Rashi*—you waited for your
friend because of My mitzvah to do kindness for others],
your peace will be like that of a river, and your righteous-
ness will be like the waves of the sea, and your children
will be [numerous] like the sand.'"

Tosafos points out that in the times of the Gemara, the shuls
were in the field, and it was therefore more important that one wait

for one's friend who was still davening. Nonetheless, *Tosafos* says that Rabbeinu Tam himself used to wait for anyone still davening before leaving the shul, and that it is "*na'eh l'hachmir*—fitting to be stringent" (but more literally, "beautiful to be stringent") for us as well, even though our shuls are inside the city. The choice of the words "*na'eh l'hachmir*" is uncommon, and is reminiscent of a Gemara at the beginning of *Masechta Nazir*. The first Mishnah in *Nazir* teaches that if one says, "*Ehei na'eh* (I will be beautiful)," his intent is to accept upon himself the status of a *nazir*. The Gemara questions that perhaps his intent was to beautify himself by the performance of other mitzvos. The Gemara answers that he was holding his hair at the time, and it is clear that his intent was to become a *nazir*. If not for this, however, one who says, "I will be beautiful" would be understood to mean that he will beautify himself with the performance of mitzvos.[1]

There is a glory and a beauty that comes with the performance of all mitzvos, but *middos tovos*, and especially the trait of humility, bring with them a certain *chein* that is almost tangible. Shlomo HaMelech writes in *Mishlei*, "To the humble, He gives *chein*,"[2] and "Humility precedes honor"[3] (i.e., people love and honor those who are humble). Imagine how we would feel toward Rabbeinu Tam if we came late to davening, finished *Shemoneh Esreh* long after the rest of the community, and noticed that Rabbeinu Tam himself was waiting for us to finish out of sensitivity that we shouldn't feel that we are all alone. Such humility! Someone so great and busy as Rabbeinu Tam has such sensitivity to do this for me! It's beautiful! And it's "*na'eh*" for us to be stringent as well!

We can apply this sensitivity and this willingness to sacrifice some of our time for others in many situations that arise. The ability to do this arises from the beautiful trait of humility.

Humility and sensitivity to others are beautiful traits.

---

1   *Nazir* 2b.
2   *Mishlei* 3:34.
3   Ibid., 15:33.

6a

SEE THE BENEFITS OF YOUR LIMITATIONS

תניא, אבא בנימין אומר: אלמלי נתנה רשות לעין
לראות, אין כל בריה יכולה לעמוד מפני המזיקין.

Abba Binyamin says, "If we would have the ability to see
the numerous dangerous spiritual beings that surround
us, we would not be able to endure it."

There are times when our limitations are to our benefit. The *Chovos Halevavos* in *Shaar Habechinah* mentions the following human limitations and explains how they are all for our benefit.

- If a young child was aware of how dependent he is on others for all of his basic needs, he would be overcome by worry and sorrow.
- If not for the trait of forgetfulness, a person who even once had reason to be sad would remain sad for their entire life.
- If not for the trait of bashfulness, people would commit many more sins.
- If not for darkness and the inability to see at night, people would push themselves to the point of destruction by working constantly, day and night.

This concept is applicable to each of us individually as well. We all have limitations. Sometimes we wish that we didn't need to struggle in a particular area. It isn't always easy to realize how the limitation is actually for our benefit.

The Steipler Gaon writes that a *talmid* who has limited intellectual ability and struggles to understand what he is learning

> *should not be frustrated or unhappy. To the contrary, because learning does not come easily to him, when he finally does grasp it and it becomes anchored in his mind, he will experience a greater joy from his accomplishment, and as a result it will remain more firmly embedded in his memory. The difficulties one encounters in the course of Torah learning ultimately lead to greater joy in one's success and to a greater attachment to Torah.*[1]

Don't let your limitations make you feel down. Contemplate how you may even benefit from some of them.

---

1   Translated in *Rav Pam: The Life and Ideals of Rabbi Avrohom Yaakov Pam* by Rabbi Shimon Finkelman, from *Birkas Peretz, Parashas Lech Lecha*.

6a

SHOW APPRECIATION

הני תפילין דמרי עלמא מה כתיב בהו? אמר ליה: ומי
כעמך ישראל גוי אחד בארץ. ומי משתבח קודשא
בריך הוא בשבחייהו דישראל? אין, דכתיב: את ה'
האמרת היום (וכתיב) וה' האמירך היום.

[Having learned that Hashem himself wears tefillin
(so to speak), the Gemara says:] Which *parshiyos* are
contained in His tefillin?..."Who is like your nation
Yisrael?"...Does Hashem truly take pride in the greatness of the Jewish People? Yes, as the *pasuk* says, "You
have declared Hashem as a unique Object of praise and
importance, and Hashem has declared you as a unique
object of praise and importance."

Hashem's tefillin bespeak the high regard that Hashem feels
toward us. Hashem, the all-powerful Creator of the entire world, takes
great pride in being associated with us. Not only does Hashem feel
this way, He even "openly expresses" it by wearing tefillin that contain
this idea.

Hashem does not have a physical body on which to don tefillin. What
does it mean that Hashem wears tefillin?

Perhaps it is a way of emphasizing that Hashem openly expresses His respect for the Jewish People. The Mishnah in *Pirkei Avos* teaches us, "The Jewish People are beloved...Hashem showed them additional affection by telling them that they are beloved."[1] This additional affection is emphasized when Hashem wears tefillin that bespeak our greatness.

At the beginning of *Parashas Noach*, the Torah tells us that Noach is perfectly righteous. When Hashem speaks with Noach, however, He says, "I have seen that you are righteous." *Rashi* notices that here the *pasuk* does not say "perfectly righteous" as the earlier verse did, and explains that this is because one should only say some of a person's praise when speaking with them directly.[2] (*Rashi* explains that this is because excessive praise appears to be mere flattery.[3] The *Maharsha* disagrees and explains that it is to avoid making the listener feel conceited.)

Rav Hadar Margolin, in *Shiras Halev*, points out that *Rashi* is teaching us two points. First, that we should not praise a person excessively when speaking directly to him, and second, that one should go out of the way to make sure to say *some* of the other person's praise. It is very important to let someone know how highly you think of them. It will bring them joy and it will motivate them to accomplish great things.[4]

Dale Carnegie writes: "Let's try to figure out the other person's good points. Then forget flattery. Give honest, sincere appreciation. Be 'hearty in your approbation and lavish in your praise,' and people will cherish your words and treasure them, and repeat them over a lifetime—repeat them years after you have forgotten them."[5]

Compliment sincerely and show people that you appreciate them.

---

1   *Avos* 3:14.
2   *Bereishis* 7:1.
3   *Rashi, Eruvin* 18b.
4   P. 184.
5   Dale Carnegie, *How to Win Friends and Influence People*, p. 29.

6b

GROWTH TAKES EFFORT

אמר רבין בר רב אדא אמר רבי יצחק: כל הרגיל לבא
לבית הכנסת ולא בא יום אחד—הקדוש ברוך הוא
משאיל בו, שנאמר: מי בכם ירא ה' שמע בקול עבדו
אשר הלך חשכים ואין נגה לו.

Ravin bar Rav Addah said in the name of Rabbi Yitzchak,
"Anyone who is accustomed to coming to shul and one
day does not come, Hashem inquires about him, as it
says, 'Which of you fears Hashem and listens to the voice
of His servant? Though he may have walked in darkness
without light for himself.'"[1]

Rashi explains that when the *pasuk* refers to "having walked in
darkness," it means that the person "went to a place of darkness and
didn't come early to the shul." The *pasuk* continues by saying that he
has "no light for himself." One who doesn't invest in going to a place
of "light" is left without it. In matters of spirituality, the benefits are
a direct outgrowth of the effort invested. This is not to say that there

---

1   *Yeshayahu* 50:10.

must be "difficulty" or a sense of pushing through a "chore." Effort can be enjoyable and a pleasure, but there must be effort.

The Gemara in *Megillah* teaches that Torah study requires effort.[2] The Gemara in *Rosh Hashanah* teaches that successful *tefillah* requires concentration.[3] The *Mesilas Yesharim* teaches that "to the degree to which one conquered one's evil inclination and desires, and distanced the impediments to doing good, and attached oneself to good, to that degree will he attain it and derive joy from it."[4]

John Maxwell writes:

> *When we are children, our bodies grow automatically. A year goes by, and we become taller, stronger, more capable of doing new things and facing new challenges. I think many people carry into adulthood a subconscious belief that mental, spiritual, and emotional growth follows a similar pattern...No one improves by accident. Personal growth doesn't just happen on its own. And once you're done with your formal education, you must take complete ownership of the growth process, because nobody else will do it for you. If you want your life to improve, you must improve yourself.*[5]

Growth doesn't happen automatically. You have to invest the effort.

---

2   *Megillah* 6b.
3   *Rosh Hashanah* 18a
4   *Mesilas Yesharim*, introduction.
5   John Maxwell, *How Successful People Grow*, p. 2.

6b

THE HUMILITY TO CONCEDE

אמר רבי זירא: מריש כי הוה חזינא להו לרבנן דקא
רהטי לפרקא בשבתא, אמינא: קא מחליין רבנן
שבתא. כיון דשמענא להא דרבי תנחום אמר רבי
יהושע בן לוי: לעולם ירוץ אדם לדבר הלכה ואפילו
בשבת, שנאמר אחרי ה' ילכו כאריה ישאג וגו'—אנא
נמי רהיטנא.

Rabbi Zeira said: Originally, when I would see the rabbis
running to a *shiur* on Shabbos, I would say, "The rabbis
are desecrating the Shabbos." Once I heard the teaching of Rabbi Tanchum in the name of Rabbi Yehoshua
ben Levi that one should always run to a *shiur* even on
Shabbos, as it says, "They will walk after Hashem like a
lion that roars," I also ran [to the *shiur*].

Rabbi Zeira believed that the rabbis who ran to the *shiur* on
Shabbos were desecrating the Shabbos. Because desecrating Shabbos is
so severe, Rabbi Zeira must have had strong negative feelings about this
practice. Usually, when someone has strong feelings about something,
it is not easy for them to change their mind. Nonetheless, as soon as
Rabbi Zeira learned the teaching that one should run to hear Torah even

on Shabbos, he began to run as well. He did not feel the need to defend his strongly held opinion. He was concerned only by what was right.

The Gemara in *Sanhedrin* teaches us that Rabbi Zeira, in his great humility, would hide to avoid receiving *semichah*. He only agreed to receive *semichah* after he learned that one who is elevated is forgiven for all of his sins. At the time that he received *semichah*, the people sang a short song comparing him to a bride who is beautiful without makeup.[1] The *Maharsha* explains that there were people at the time who would fake piety. They would dress externally like the pious but were not, in fact, righteous at all. The song that they sang for Rabbi Zeira was to emphasize that he was truly pious and was not like those who merely "put on makeup," i.e., pretending to be pious. He was the type of person who was interested solely in what was right and not in what others would think about him. This is the trait of one who will readily concede when they learn that their strongly held opinion is not correct.

Have the humility to concede. Don't let your pride interfere
with recognizing truth.

---

1 *Sanhedrin* 14a.

6b

RECOGNIZE THE ELEMENTS OF SUCCESS IN FAILURE

אמר רבי זירא: אגרא דפרקא—רהטא.

Rabbi Zeira said: The reward for going to a *shiur* is [primarily] for the running to the *shiur*.

Rashi explains that most people who go to hear a *derashah* will not receive reward for the learning itself. They will not have the understanding or the ability to repeat later what they learned, and so they cannot be considered to have actually learned the subject matter. (This is not to say that one without an exceptional memory or academic ability can't learn. If the people would review what they learned, they would understand and remember it, and they would receive reward for the learning.) The primary reward that they receive is for the enthusiasm with which they ran to hear the *derashah*.

Imagine someone who runs enthusiastically to hear a *derashah*, sits intently throughout the *derashah*, and returns home only to find that after several hours he has already forgotten what he has learned. Imagine if he was aware that the primary credit for learning is not attained if it is forgotten immediately. It would be so disheartening. The person may think, "All that effort and it was a failure." They may overlook the fact that sometimes things that appear to have been a failure produce other benefits that are valuable as well. Actions shouldn't be judged based on one aspect alone. Even if one aspect of an endeavor fails, the endeavor may not have been a total failure. While the person may not receive the primary credit for learning, they nonetheless receive the reward for enthusiastically running to the *shiur* and demonstrating that love for Hashem and His Torah.

Robert Leahy relates the following story:

> *A young executive is handed a project by the president of the company. A year later, the project is scrapped after millions have been spent. The president calls the young executive into his office. The executive is worried: "Will I lose my job? I failed on this enormous responsibility. He's going to think I'm a loser." However, the president says, "Dan, I've got a new project for you. In fact, it's even bigger than the last one." Dan is relieved but a bit confused, and he says to the president, "I'm really happy to get this new project. But to be honest with you, I expected you to fire me after I failed on that last project." The president replied: "Fire you? I wouldn't fire you after I've spent millions on your education!" What the president is focusing on is what the young executive learned and how he can apply it on the next project.[1]*

The lesson of the story is that even what appears to be a complete failure may in fact contain elements of success that can be recognized and appreciated.

Notice the elements of success even amidst a failure.

---

1   *The Worry Cure*, p. 139.

6b

PERSONAL AND COMMUNAL GROWTH

אמר רב הונא: כל המתפלל אחורי בית הכנסת
נקרא רשע, שנאמר: סביב רשעים יתהלכון.
אמר אביי: לא אמרן אלא דלא מהדר אפיה
לבי כנישתא, אבל מהדר אפיה לבי כנישתא —
לית לן בה.

Rav Huna teaches that one who davens behind the shul
is considered to be wicked. Abaye explains that this is
only if he does not turn around to face the shul.

Tosafos quotes *Rashi* (which is different from our text in *Rashi*) as explaining that in Bavel, one would enter the shul through a doorway in the east. The community would daven facing west. The doorway was considered to be the front of the shul, and the direction the community faced was considered to be the back of the shul. One who would stand "behind the shul," without turning around to face the shul, would have his back to the community and the *Aron Kodesh*. This is the Gemara's intent when it describes "davening behind the shul."

Tosafos argues that this cannot be the explanation of the Gemara. A person davening in this way is facing the same direction as the

47

community. This is the appropriate way to daven. On the contrary, if he were to turn around and face the shul, it would be problematic. Then he would be davening in the opposite direction from everyone else. *Tosafos* therefore explains that the person who is "davening behind the shul" is standing in the east, near the entrance to the shul, and facing away from the shul. Thus, he is both facing away from the shul and davening in the opposite direction from the community.

We now have a *machlokes* between *Rashi* and *Tosafos* in a case where one is standing on the west side of the shul (in Bavel, where they davened facing west). *Rashi* says that he should face the shul and the community. *Tosafos* is of the opinion that he should face the same direction that the community is facing, even though that would mean turning his back to the shul.

Sometimes we find ourselves surrounded by good, growth-minded people working on bettering themselves in *avodas Hashem*, who may not be on as high a level as we find ourselves. We may be already involved in devoting our time and effort to growing on a higher plane than the others in our surroundings. Should we face upward, as the community does, and look toward growing to even greater personal heights, despite the fact that this may mean turning our back toward the community? Or should we turn toward the community and work together with them, assisting them on an aspect of spiritual growth that we have already mastered? Sometimes it is a difficult challenge to find the proper balance between these two options.

The *Pischei Teshuvah* in *Hilchos Dayanim* quotes the *Chasam Sofer* who writes:

> *A person should not pursue luxuries. The more a person is satisfied with caring for his basic needs, thus increasing the time that he can spend studying Torah and serving Hashem, the holier he is. If during the time that a person has designated for his personal study, someone approaches him to learn Torah from him or to ask him to adjudicate a monetary dispute, he*

must do so free of charge. Even though he is losing out on his own learning, his friend takes priority.[1]

We see from here that, at times, we must sacrifice our own growth in order to help others grow.

This does not mean that we should focus exclusively on helping others and entirely ignore our own growth. If we did this, we would shortly find that we no longer have anything else to give. We have to work on our own growth so that we will have what to share.

Rav Wolbe writes in *Alei Shur*, "Chazal say, 'Moshe merited and enabled others to merit.'[2] This is the way: Only what one has acquired for oneself, and areas in which one has purified [i.e., perfected] oneself—in this one can enable the community to grow as well."[3]

Balance your striving for personal growth with assisting others and communal growth.

---

1   *Piskei Teshuvah, Choshen Mishpat* 9:8.
2   *Avos* 5:18.
3   *Alei Shur*, vol. 1, p. 264.

7a

USE YOUR STRENGTHS
AND INTERESTS TO GROW

מאי מצלי? אמר רב זוטרא בר טוביה אמר רב: יהי רצון מלפני שיכבשו רחמי את כעסי, ויגולו רחמי על מדותי, ואתנהג עם בני במדת רחמים, ואכנס להם לפנים משורת הדין. תניא, אמר רבי ישמעאל בן אלישע: פעם אחת נכנסתי להקטיר קטורת לפני ולפנים, וראיתי אכתריא-ל י-ה ה' צבאו-ת שהוא יושב על כסא רם ונשא ואמר לי: ישמעאל בני, ברכני! אמרתי לו: יהי רצון מלפניך שיכבשו רחמיך את כעסך ויגולו רחמיך על מדותיך ותתנהג עם בניך במדת הרחמים ותכנס להם לפנים משורת הדין, ונענע לי בראשו.

What is Hashem's *tefillah*? Rav Zutra bar Tuvia says in the name of Rav, "May it be My will that My mercy will conquer My anger and overcome all of My other traits, and that I should interact with My children with the trait of mercy and leniency beyond the letter of the law on their behalf." Rabbi Yishmael ben Elisha says, "I once entered the *Kodesh Hakodashim* to bring the incense offering. I saw Hashem seated on an elevated throne. He said to me, 'Yishmael, My son, bless Me.' I said to Him, 'May it be Your will that Your mercy conquers Your anger and overcome all of Your other traits, and may You interact with Your children with the trait of mercy, and leniency beyond the letter of the law on their behalf.' He nodded His head [in approval]."

Rabbi Yishmael blessed Hashem with a *berachah* that was identical to Hashem's *tefillah*. Of course, blessing Hashem is of a different nature than human relationships, but perhaps on some level we can learn from here that it is most valuable to encourage someone in the area where they already feel connected and motivated. If we try to motivate someone in an area that they don't value, they will not be interested in our encouragement. Effective education requires determining what is important to the person, how specifically they can grow in that area of their interest, and how that can become a springboard for growth in a variety of areas.

The same is true when we focus on our own personal growth. The first questions that we can ask ourselves are "What is most important to me?" and "What are my strengths?" We can then encourage ourselves to grow in the areas that we value using our strengths and positive qualities. We can then ask ourselves how we can use this growth to develop in other areas as well.

Grow in areas that are important to you and where you find your strengths. Enable others to do the same.

7a

SCHEDULE ANGER TIME

ואימת רתח?

[The Gemara tells us that Hashem becomes angry for one moment every day. The Gemara then asks,] "And when does He grow angry?"

Hashem has a specific time of day when he "becomes angry." Why does Hashem select the same moment every day? Wouldn't it make more sense to become angry at the time that humanity sins, which would be at a different time every day? Even if Hashem wants to limit His "anger" to a moment, the moment could be selected based on the greatest amount of sin on any given day.

One component of cognitive therapy for General Anxiety Disorder (GAD) is scheduling "worry time." Setting aside a specific time each day to worry accomplishes two primary goals of treatment. The first is that frequently, those suffering from GAD view worry as uncontrollable. When a person is able to push aside worry throughout the day by saving it for later, he realizes that he does have a degree of control over his worries. The second benefit is that people with GAD sometimes think that they worry about many different things. Frequently, many of their worries revolve around the same theme and are really just repetitions of the same worry. When they engage in "worry time," they are able

52

to recognize that their worries are mainly repetitive. They can then address the theme of their worry directly without feeling overwhelmed by a multitude of worries.

The same benefits can be derived from scheduling "anger time." Rather than allowing an anger thought to snowball into a strong emotion of anger, one can save the thought and anger for their scheduled anger time. The multiple benefits of this approach include the ability to see that anger really is controllable, and that frequently, the underlying themes of one's anger are related. It will then be possible to work on that theme without feeling overwhelmed by a broad and general sense of anger. While anger and worry are traits that should ideally be conquered entirely (anger through working on humility, and worry through working on trust in Hashem), this method can be helpful in working toward that elevated goal.

Perhaps it is in order to teach us this lesson that Hashem directs His anger at the same one pre-scheduled moment of every day.

Scheduling anger time or worry time can be helpful in minimizing the intensity and frequency of these negative emotions.

7a

INSPIRE YOURSELF
AND ENABLE OTHERS
TO INSPIRE THEMSELVES

וְאָמַר רַבִּי יוֹחָנָן מִשּׁוּם רַבִּי יוֹסֵי: טוֹבָה מַרְדוּת אַחַת
בְּלִבּוֹ שֶׁל אָדָם יוֹתֵר מִכַּמָּה מַלְקִיּוֹת.

One powerful internal feeling of self-rebuke is more
effective than intense physical coercion from others.

The ability to inspire oneself has many advantages over the need
to find inspiration from others. Of course, we should eagerly pursue
opportunities to hear inspiration, but the greatest inspiration is what
we obtain from within ourselves.

There are two reasons why this is so:

- Rabbeinu Yonah comments on the Mishnah that teaches, "If I
  am not for myself, who will be for me?"[1] that inspiration from
  others is limited to the few times when others provide it. It cannot be compared to the constant inspiration that we can provide
  for ourselves and carry with us at all times.

---

1   *Avos* 1:14.

- The second advantage of inspiring ourselves is that we will feel a personal connection to the message. Chazal teach that a person prefers to have one measure of his own produce than nine measures of produce obtained from someone else.[2] We feel connected to what is ours.

The value of inspiring ourselves is also an important tool for educators and parents to keep in mind. If we can instill in students the feeling that their inspiration is from within, it can be very motivating.

The *Chovos Hatalmidim* writes:

> It is insufficient to teach the child that he is obligated to obey his teachers...for this alone will not help. Eventually, the child will see his rebbi as his opposition, as almost a dictator. The most important element is to instill in the child the understanding that he himself is his own primary teacher. He is not merely a child. He is a sapling, planted by Hashem, in the vineyard of the Jewish People. And Hashem placed upon him the responsibility to raise and educate himself to grow into a big tree, the tree of life, as a servant of Hashem, righteous, and great in Torah...The parents and teachers are only instructors guiding the child in the way that he should educate himself.[3]

Dale Carnegie writes: "No one likes to feel that he or she is being sold something or told to do a thing. We much prefer to feel that we are buying of our own accord or acting on our own ideas. We like to be consulted about our wishes, our wants, our thoughts...Letting the other person feel that the idea is his or her's works in business, politics, and family life as well."[4]

Inspire yourself. Allow others the joy and motivation of feeling that they are guiding their own education and decisions.

---

2   *Bava Metzia* 38a.

3   *Chovos Hatalmidim*, chap. 1, "A Conversation with Teachers, Parents, and Children."

4   *Win Friends and Influence People*, p. 156.

7a

THE RISK OF LOST OPPORTUNITY

תנא משמיה דרבי יהושע בן קרחה, כך אמר לו
הקדוש ברוך הוא למשה: כשרציתי לא רצית, עכשיו
שאתה רוצה—איני רוצה.

The *Beraisa* teaches in the name of Rabbi Yehoshua ben
Korcha, "Hashem said to Moshe, 'When I wanted, you did
not. Now that you want, I do not.'"

When Hashem appeared to Moshe Rabbeinu in the burning bush,
Moshe Rabbeinu had an amazing opportunity. The *Baal Haturim* says
that not only would he have been able to "see" Hashem, but he also
would have been able to daven for the Jewish People at such an oppor-
tune moment that they never would have been exiled again. He turned
down the opportunity and it was not made available to him later.[1]

Why did Moshe turn down the opportunity? The *pasuk* tells us that he
was afraid. While many interpret this fear as a calculated decision that
it would be inappropriate to gaze at the *Shechinah*, these interpretations presumably follow the opinion of Tanna'im that Moshe Rabbeinu
made the correct decision in turning away and was later rewarded for it.

---

1   *Shemos* 3:6.

However, the opinion in the Gemara that suggests that Moshe should not have turned away would likely interpret the *pasuk* literally—that Moshe Rabbeinu feared gazing at the *Shechinah*. Perhaps he was concerned that there was a risk involved. Hashem himself says, "For man cannot see My face and live."[2] It is not a small matter to gaze at the *Shechinah*, and Moshe was hesitant. While Moshe's fear is understandable, he lost out on a once-in-history opportunity.

When one avoids a situation out of fear, one is choosing the more comfortable option. One calculates the pros and cons of the situation and decides on the alternative that is more comfortable. Unfortunately, one factor that is frequently overlooked is "opportunity cost," or what could be accomplished if one confronts the fear and chooses to act.

Robert Leahy writes: "Many people are hesitant to make decisions because they believe there is a risk involved and that not making a decision will avoid the risk...In making decisions, the rational view would be to weigh the risk of deciding versus the risk of not deciding. There is no risk-free alternative, so the individual may need to weigh the cost of lost opportunities in not deciding."[3]

Don't miss out on an opportunity. Balance the risk involved in trying with the risk of losing out if you remain passive.

---

2   Ibid., 33:20.
3   Robert Leahy, *Cognitive Therapy Techniques*, p. 206.

7b

GRATITUDE

ואמר רבי יוחנן משום רבי שמעון בן יוחי: מיום
שברא הקדוש ברוך הוא את עולמו לא היה אדם
שהודה להקדוש ברוך הוא עד שבאתה לאה והודתו,
שנאמר הפעם אודה את ה'.

Rabbi Yochanan said in the name of Rabbi Shimon Bar Yochai, "From the day that Hashem created His world, nobody offered thanks to Him until Leah came and thanked Him, as it says, 'This time I shall thank Hashem.'"

Rashi explains that Leah saw with *ruach ha'kodesh* that Yaakov would have twelve sons. Since Yaakov had four wives, each wife would have three sons. When Leah had Yehudah, her fourth son, she felt that she had been given more than she was entitled to, and she was inspired to thank Hashem.

The *Chovos Halevavos* lists three impediments that hinder our feelings of gratefulness to Hashem. They are:

1. Over-involvement in worldly matters and the constant pursuit of physical pleasures
2. Growing accustomed to the kindness that Hashem does for us

3. The various forms of suffering in this world that befall all people.[1]

The *Chovos Halevavos* elaborates on the second impediment by relating the following parable. A kind man once found a baby all alone in the desert. He took him into his home, raised him, fed him, and clothed him. He provided him with all of his needs throughout his childhood. The kind man then heard of a prisoner who had been taken captive by the enemy and had suffered severely under his captors. The kind man went to plead with the captors and succeeded in freeing the prisoner. He brought him into his home and provided him with only a fraction of what he had bestowed on the child whom he had found and raised. Nonetheless, it was the prisoner who expressed much greater gratitude than the child. The child had grown accustomed to everything that he was given long before his intellect had fully developed and long before he could develop a true sense of gratitude. The prisoner, on the other hand, had experienced a transition from suffering to redemption at an age that he could appreciate it.

So too, explains the *Chovos Halevavos*, we come into this world as a baby, unable to appreciate everything that Hashem created for us and that He does for us. When our minds develop, we have already become so accustomed to everything that we no longer appreciate it all. It takes a greater effort to recognize that we aren't truly entitled to our "expectations," and that we should feel grateful for everything that we are accustomed to.

At the beginning of *Parashas Va'eschanan*, Moshe davens to Hashem to ask for permission to enter Eretz Yisrael. *Rashi* points out that the word "*va'eschanan*" connotes that Moshe asked Hashem for a free gift. Even though the righteous could ask Hashem for reward for the mitzvos that they have performed, instead they ask Hashem for a "free gift."

The *Kli Yakar* questions, "How can the righteous ask for good in this world as reward for the mitzvos that they have performed? Hashem is never indebted to a person. All of the mitzvos that a person performs

---

1   *Chovos Halevavos, Shaar Habechinah*, introduction.

cannot properly repay Hashem for all of the kindness that He has already done for them."

Perhaps the answer to the *Kli Yakar*'s question is that this statement of Chazal—"Even though the righteous could ask [for goodness] as a reward for their good deeds, instead they ask for it as a free gift"—is intended to teach the point of the *Kli Yakar*. The righteous realize that even though they have performed many mitzvos—and therefore on a superficial level, they could ask for reward—when contemplating everything that Hashem does for them, they understand that on a deeper level they aren't really "entitled" to anything. Hence, they ask Hashem not for reward but for a free gift.

Stan Toler writes: "The most happy and successful people are keenly aware that life—and everything in it—is undeserved. They see themselves as blessed and fortunate, and they practice the attitude of gratitude. That positive awareness results in a feeling of gratefulness, a lighter spirit, and a willingness to give to others."[2]

A feeling of entitlement decreases gratitude. To enjoy the true feeling of gratitude, decrease your feelings of entitlement.

---

2   Stan Toler, *The Power of Your Attitude*, p. 91.

7b

JUDGE FAVORABLY

אמר רבי שמעון בן אבישלום.

[The Gemara quotes a Torah scholar by the name of]
Rabbi Shimon ben Avishalom.

The Gemara in *Yoma* teaches that one may not name a child after someone who is wicked.[1] David HaMelech's evil son Avshalom led a rebellion against him, and, as such, Avshalom is certainly a forbidden name. The *Mesores Hashas* notes that the name "Avishalom" in our Gemara resembles the name "Avshalom." The *Mesores Hashas* then cites *Tosafos*, who differentiates between the name "Avishalom" and "Avshalom." Avishalom is not the same person as Avshalom, and therefore it is permitted.

The smallest difference in a person can drastically affect how we perceive them. If we see someone as an "Avshalom" but we're missing just one *yud*, i.e., one aspect of their life or their character that we don't know about, our entire perception of them may be mistaken.

Stephen Covey relates the following powerful story that illustrates how it is impossible to evaluate someone, as there is always information that we are missing.

---

1   *Yoma* 38b.

I remember a mini-paradigm shift I experienced one Sunday morning on a subway in New York. People were sitting quietly…It was a calm, peaceful scene. Then suddenly, a man and his children entered the subway car. The children were so loud and rambunctious that instantly the whole climate changed…It was difficult not to feel irritated. I could not believe that he could be so insensitive as to let his children run wild like that and do nothing about it…I turned to him and said, "Sir, your children are really disturbing a lot of people. I wonder if you couldn't control them a little more?" The man lifted his gaze as if to come to a consciousness of the situation for the first time and said softly, "Oh, you're right. I guess I should do something about it. We just came from the hospital where their mother died about an hour ago. I don't know what to think, and I guess they don't know how to handle it either."[2]

Even if we are only missing a detail, a little *yud*, a component of a person's life that may be hidden to us, our entire outlook toward them may be mistaken. It is for this reason that the Mishnah in *Avos* teaches us to "judge the entire person as meritorious."[3] If we were to know the entire person, our perception of them would be positive.

Don't judge someone until you know every aspect of their life.
If that is not possible, judge them favorably.

---

2   *Seven Habits*, p. 38.

3   *Avos* 1:6.

7b

RECOGNIZING YOUR ABILITY TO COPE

אדם שיצא עליו שטר חוב, קודם שפרעו היה עצב,
לאחר שפרעו שמח.

A person who owed a debt was sad before he repaid it.
After he repaid it, however, he rejoiced.

When people are worried about a debt that they owe, they are saddened. After they repay the debt, they are happy. Why is this? They were worried about losing the money that they felt they needed, and when they are in the situation of actually having lost the money, they feel a lot better. This is difficult to understand.

Anxiety is caused by a combination of overestimating the risk of a situation and underestimating one's ability to cope. When a person worries about a debt that they must repay, they think that they will have difficulty managing this loss of money. After they repay the debt, they see that they are, in fact, able to cope quite well, and the anxiety decreases.

When we worry about things, we frequently focus on one specific point in time. We don't think about what will happen after the occurrence of what we are worried about. Robert Leahy writes:

Take Elvin, who worries about his investments doing poorly. Right now, he seems obsessed with his loss of money, and he projects disaster into the future. But the next time I see him—the next week—he is talking about having a good time with his wife, cooking dinner at home. Events take over, and the narrow focus on the worry is eventually lost. Imagine getting into a time machine. Go into the future a week, two weeks, a month, or a year. Almost everything that you worry about today will seem trivial when you look back on it from the future. This is quite informative, because it tells us that many of the things that bother us now turn out to be unimportant.[1]

Decrease your anxiety by picturing the future and seeing how well you are able to cope.

---

1   *The Worry Cure*, p. 187.

8a

FIND A ROLE MODEL

ואמר רבי חייא בר אמי משמיה דעולא: לעולם ידור
אדם במקום רבו, שכל זמן ששמעי בן גרא קיים לא
נשא שלמה את בת פרעה.

A person should always live near his *rebbi*, for as long
as Shimi ben Geira [Shlomo HaMelech's *rebbi*] was living,
[Shlomo HaMelech] did not marry Pharaoh's daughter.

Living near a mentor can have a profound impact on a person. The
more time that you spend with people of exemplary character, the more
likely it is that you will mold your own character in a similar way.

The *Rambam* teaches us that "it is the nature of man for one's character to be influenced by his friends and townspeople. It is therefore
necessary to develop friendships with the righteous and to spend time
with the wise in order to learn from their ways."[1]

John Maxwell writes:

> We become like the people we admire and the models we follow.
> For that reason, we should take great care when determining
> which people we ask to mentor us. They must not only display

---

1   *Rambam, Mishneh Torah, De'os* 6:1.

professional excellence and possess skill sets from which we can learn, they must also demonstrate character worthy of emulating...For us to be able to observe models up close and see what they do, we must have some contact with them. That requires access and availability. For us to be actively mentored, we must have time with people to ask questions and learn from their answers.[2]

Find an exemplary role model to emulate.

---

2   *How Succesful People Grow*, p. 116.

8b

THE BENEFITS
OF A TORAH LIFESTYLE

כל האוכל ושותה בתשיעי—מעלה עליו הכתוב
כאילו מתענה תשיעי ועשירי.

Anyone who eats and drinks on the ninth day of Tishrei
[Erev Yom Kippur] is considered as if he fasted on both
the ninth and tenth days.

There is a difference of opinion as to why one should eat on Erev
Yom Kippur. According to *Rashi*, it is so that one will have strength to
fast on Yom Kippur.[1] Rabbeinu Yonah suggests three additional reasons. One reason is in order to show our joy over our forgiveness on the
next day. The second reason is that since we can't have a *seudas yom tov*
(holiday meal) on Yom Kippur, as it is a fast day, the *seudah* is enjoyed
the day before Yom Kippur instead. The third reason is to strengthen
ourselves in preparation for the long Yom Kippur davening.[2]

According to Rabbeinu Yonah's second reason, the meal on Erev Yom
Kippur is the Yom Tov feast that would normally be enjoyed on Yom

---

1   *Rashi, Yoma* 81b.
2   *Shaarei Teshuvah* 4:8–10.

Tov. It is about this feast that our Gemara teaches us that one who feasts on the ninth of Tishrei will be rewarded as if he had fasted two consecutive days. Hashem commands us to feast and enjoy—and then He rewards us for doing so!

The *pasuk* in *Shir Hashirim* says, "His palate [i.e., His words] is sweet and He is entirely a delight."[3] *Rashi* comments, "Hashem commands us not to injure ourselves and then promises us reward for obeying. Is there anything sweeter than that?"[4]

The mitzvos of the Torah are all for our benefit, but not only do we benefit from fulfilling them, we are even rewarded as well. It is worthwhile to think about the *mitzvos haTorah* and how much we gain from leading a Torah lifestyle. *Menuchas Shabbos*, time together with family, freedom from many of the ills of society, a connection to spirituality, a sense of gratitude and happiness that stems from satisfaction and purpose—these are just a few of the things that a Torah lifestyle grants us. Try to compile your own list of how you benefit from a Torah lifestyle.

Think about the beauty and peacefulness of a Torah lifestyle.

---

3   *Shir Hashirim* 5:16.
4   *Vayikra* 19.

8b

REMORSE AND NOT GUILT

הזהרו בזקן ששכח תלמודו מחמת אונסו, דאמרינן:
לוחות ושברי לוחות מונחות בארון.

Take care to respect an elder who forgot his learning
due to reasons beyond his control, for we have learned
that both the *luchos* and the broken *luchos* were placed
in the *Aron*.

Rabbi Moshe Weinberger related the following *mashal* in the
name of Rav Chatzkel Levenstein: A man builds a beautiful palace, and
upon its completion he stands atop the roof admiring his masterpiece.
Caught up in his thoughts, he slips and falls from the roof. When he
regains consciousness, he finds himself in a hospital bed. Not knowing
exactly what happened at the time of his injury, he begins to bemoan
the collapse of his palace. His friend who is visiting him in the hospital
comforts him and informs him that the palace did not collapse, and
as soon as he regains his strength, he will return to his intact beautiful palace.

Rav Levenstein explained that the same is true in our *avodas Hashem*.
We work hard to create a beautiful palace of Torah, mitzvos, and devotion to Hashem. Unfortunately, we sometimes fall. Mistakenly, we

believe that our entire palace has been demolished. That is not the case. The palace remains intact. It is only that we have fallen from it. Once we pick ourselves up and regain our strength, we return directly to the beautiful and intact palace that we have built.

The Torah says, "Any [fish] that has fins and scales in the water, the seas, or the streams, those you may eat."[1] From here, Chazal teach us that a fish that has fins and scales when it is in the water, but loses them when it emerges from the water, is still a kosher fish. Rabbi Weinberger explained that sometimes we find ourselves in an environment filled with the life of Torah, represented by water. We are successful, and we find ourselves on a high spiritual level. There are times when we later discover ourselves in an environment outside the waters of Torah. We experience a decline and lose our *"simanei kashrus."* It is essential that we understand that we are still "kosher." Even the broken *luchos* retain their holiness and are safeguarded in the *Aron Hakodesh*.

When mistakes that we make lead us to feel less about ourselves, we fall into the trap of succumbing to guilt. Dr. David Burns writes:

> *The concept of the "badness" of self is central to guilt. In its absence, your hurtful action might lead to a healthy feeling of remorse but not guilt. Remorse stems from the undistorted awareness that you have willfully and unnecessarily acted in a hurtful manner toward yourself or another person that violates your personal ethical standards. Remorse differs from guilt because there is no implication your transgression indicates you are inherently bad, evil, or immoral. To put it in a nutshell, remorse or regret are aimed at behavior, whereas guilt is targeted toward the "self." If in addition to your guilt you feel depression, shame, or anxiety, you are probably making one of the following assumptions. 1. Because of my "bad behavior," I am inferior or worthless (this interpretation leads to depression). 2. If others found out what I did, they would look down on me*

---

1   *Vayikra* 11:9.

(this cognition leads to shame). 3. I'm in danger of retaliation or punishment (this thought provokes anxiety).[2]

The holy *Aron* was kept in the Holy of Holies. It contained the perfect, unbroken *luchos* that Hashem gave us on Har Sinai, and next to those perfect *luchos* were the broken *luchos* that Moshe shattered upon witnessing the people violating idolatry, which is one of the most severe of prohibitions. Our Gemara teaches us that we are to derive from here that even after a fall, we remain respectable and elevated.

Don't let mistakes detract from your feeling of self-worth.

---

2   Dr. David Burns, *Feeling Good,* p. 199.

8b

MOTIVATE YOURSELF POSITIVELY

והזהרו בזקן ששכח תלמודו מחמת אונסו.

Be careful to show respect for an elder who forgot his
learning due to causes beyond his control.

Rashi explains that when the Gemara refers to one who forgot his
learning due to something beyond his control, this includes one who
needed to take time away from his learning in order to make a living.
The Gemara tells us that he is entitled to respect. He is entitled to respect from others, and he is entitled to self-respect as well.

The *Shulchan Aruch* in *hilchos Talmud Torah* teaches that in cases of
necessity one can fulfill one's basic obligation to learn Torah by saying
Shema in the morning and in the evening.[1] There is a dispute in *Masechta
Menachos* (99b) as to whether one should inform people of this leniency.
The *Shach paskens* like the opinion that one should inform people. *Rashi*
on the Gemara explains the rationale behind this opinion. He writes
that informing people will actually encourage them to increase their
learning. They will say to themselves, "We know of the great reward
that one receives for fulfilling one's obligation to learn Torah. If this is
accomplished by merely saying *Shema*, we can only imagine the great

---

1   *Shulchan Aruch, Yoreh Deah* 246.

reward that one merits for learning additional Torah." This positive form of motivation is superior to the motivational approach that stems from the guilt of thinking that one isn't learning as much as he should. Dr. Burns writes:

> *Your guilt-provoking thoughts lead to unproductive actions that reinforce your belief in your badness. For example, a guilt-prone neurologist was trying to prepare for her medical-board certification examination. She had difficulty studying for the test, and felt guilty about the fact that she wasn't studying. So she wasted time each night watching television while the following thoughts raced through her mind: "I shouldn't be watching TV. I should be preparing for my boards. I'm lazy. I don't deserve to be a doctor"...Like many guilt prone people, she had the idea that if she punished herself enough (i.e., with these thoughts of guilt) she would eventually get moving. Unfortunately, quite the opposite was true. Her guilt simply drained her energy and reinforced her belief that she was lazy and inadequate.[2]*

When we value something, there is a tendency to criticize ourselves for falling short of the high expectations that we feel we ought to have for ourselves. While this feeling stems from the positive value that we ascribe to the matter, it is counterproductive. We must motivate ourselves with positivity, appreciating every small accomplishment in matters of importance.

Motivate yourself with positive self-talk. Appreciate every accomplishment rather than criticizing yourself for not doing more.

---

2   *Feeling Good*, p. 204.

8b

HEALTH AND SAFETY

אמר להו רבא לבניה: כשאתם חותכין בשר—אל
תחתכו על גב היד. איכא דאמרי: משום סכנה.

Rava said to his children: When you cut meat, do not
place the meat on the back of your hand [as a cutting
board]. Some explain that this is because it is dangerous.

The Gemara in *Shabbos* relates that Rav Huna asked his son Rabbah
why he didn't go more frequently to Rav Chisda to learn from his
wise teachings. Rabbah replied that when he did go to Rav Chisda, he
merely taught him worldly matters, such as how to take care of one's
bodily needs without endangering oneself. Rav Huna exclaimed, "He
is teaching you matters of health, and you say that it is merely 'worldly
matters'? Certainly, you must go to Rav Chisda to learn from him!"[1]

Our Gemara teaches us three things that Rav Huna taught his son,
(one of which was his instruction about cutting meat.) Presumably, Rav
Huna taught his son many lessons. If these three are singled out, they
are clearly lessons that Rav Huna considered highly significant. Taking

---

1   *Shabbos* 82a.

care of one's physical well-being is something that must be prioritized and considered a value.

The *Rambam* compiled a list of things that Chazal forbade because of the danger they entail.[2] In addition to these formal prohibitions, every person is obligated to use common sense to avoid situations of danger. Rav Avigdor Miller writes:

> *There are some people who look for the mitzvah of maakeh, and learn the appropriate halachos including the proper berachah, but they may not realize that if a grandson comes to visit, and the window is a little dirty, a man should not ask his grandson to sit outside on the windowsill and clean the window from the outside. He has to understand that there is no maakeh behind his grandson who is cleaning the windows...There was a man who wanted to renovate a private home and make it into a shul, but he was afraid of the building inspectors who insisted on so many safety measures that cost extra money. The man complained and said, "Ah, we're in galus (exile)..." Why should you call the fact that the building inspector requires those things "oppression?" The Torah requires it![3]*

It is important not only to avoid situations of danger but also to lead a healthy lifestyle in order to avoid future health problems. Stephen Covey writes:

> *Exercise is one of those quadrant 2 [i.e., very important though not urgent], high leverage activities that most of us don't do consistently because it isn't urgent. And because we don't do it, sooner or later we find ourselves in quadrant 1 [i.e. dealing with things that are both important and urgent], dealing with the health problems and crises that come as a natural result of our neglect. Most of us think we don't have enough time to exercise. What a distorted paradigm! We don't have time not*

---

2   *Hilchos Rotzei'ach U'Shemiras Nefesh* 11:5.

3   *Rav Avigdor Miller Speaks*, vol. 1, p. 82.

to. We're talking about 3–6 hours a week—or a minimum of thirty minutes a day, every other day. That hardly seems an inordinate amount of time considering the tremendous benefits in terms of the impact on the other 162–165 hours of the week.[4]

The Gemara in *Bava Metzia* teaches us that if one hires porters to do a job and then reneges on the commitment, he must pay them their full salary. The Gemara questions why this is so. Normally, if one hires workers and reneges, he must pay them the amount of money that they would have willingly accepted in exchange for having the day off rather than having to work. This is always less than their working salary. The Gemara answers that porters would never accept less in order to have the day off. In fact, they prefer to work. They know that if they take the day off, they will become weaker.[5]

Exercise helps us maintain our strength and our health. It is definitely worth the time.

Take care of your health, avoid danger, and remember to exercise.

---

4   *Seven Habits*, p. 301.
5   *Bava Metzia* 77a.

8b

POSITIVE AND NEGATIVE MIND-READING

דאמר רבי יהושע בן לוי: אסור לו לאדם שיעבור
אחורי בית הכנסת בשעה שהצבור מתפללין. אמר
אביי: ולא אמרן אלא דליכא פתחא אחרינא, אבל
איכא פתחא אחרינא—לית לן בה. ולא אמרן אלא
דליכא בי כנישתא אחרינא, אבל איכא בי כנישתא
אחרינא—לית לן בה. ולא אמרן אלא דלא דרי
טונא ולא רהיט, ולא מנח תפילין, אבל איכא חד
מהנך—לית לן בה.

It is forbidden to walk behind the shul when the community is davening [because others may suspect that
he is not interested in entering to daven]. Abaye says
that this is only when the only entrance to the shul is
in the back. If there is another entrance, it is permissible [because others will assume that he intends to
enter through the other entrance]. Similarly, if there
is another shul in town, it is permissible. Additionally,
if he is carrying a package, running, or wearing tefillin,
it is permitted [because his actions do not show any

disgrace, and it is clear that he is not entering to daven
only because he is preoccupied].

When there is another entrance to the shul, one doesn't have to be
concerned that people who see him pass by the first entrance without
entering will think that he is not going to daven. They will just assume
that he intends to enter through the second entrance.

Mind-reading is one of the most common cognitive distortions that
leads to negative emotions such as sadness or anxiety. It is when "you
believe you know what others are thinking, failing to consider other,
more likely possibilities."[1] It is especially problematic when "[y]ou make
the assumption that other people are looking down on you."[2] Dr. David
Burns gives the following example, "Suppose a friend passes you on the
street and fails to say hello because he is so absorbed in his thoughts he
doesn't notice you. You might erroneously conclude, 'He is ignoring me,
so he must not like me anymore.'"

From our Gemara, we learn that people usually judge others favorably.
When they see someone walking past a shul with another entrance, it is
unlikely that they will think, "Why does he not want to daven?" As long
as there is another reasonable interpretation that is more favorable
(such as when there is a second entrance to the shul), people will think
of the more favorable interpretation. Imagine the unfortunate discomfort of one who walks by the first entrance thinking that the people
standing there are looking down at him. He would benefit greatly from
questioning this negative thought and recognizing that he is engaging
in mind-reading.

Frequently negative mind-reading stems from a core belief about
others or about yourself. If you believe that people tend to be critical
and judgmental, it is more likely that you will jump to the conclusion
that others are viewing you negatively. Similarly, if you have negative
beliefs about yourself, you will be more likely to assume that others are

---

1   Judith Beck, *Cognitive Behavioral Therapy: Basics and Beyond*, p. 181.
2   *Feeling Good*, p. 37.

aware of your perceived faults. If, however, you view people as kind and compassionate, and you view yourself positively, you will be more likely to assume that other people are judging you favorably as well.

Don't engage in mind-reading. Remember that people tend to judge others favorably.

9a

APPRECIATE THE MULTIPLE COMPONENTS OF YOUR BLESSINGS

הוציאך ה׳ אלהיך ממצרים לילה—וכי בלילה יצאו? והלא לא יצאו אלא ביום, שנאמר: ממחרת הפסח יצאו בני ישראל ביד רמה! אלא: מלמד שהתחילה להם גאולה מבערב.

"Hashem took you out of Egypt by night." Did they really depart at night? Did they not leave by day, as the *pasuk* says, "On the day following the Pesach offering, B'nei Yisrael left with a strong hand." Rather, the first *pasuk* intends to teach that the redemption began the previous evening.

The redemption from Mitzrayim took place in stages. Our Gemara tells us that we received permission to leave in the evening, but the following morning is when we actually left. The Gemara in *Rosh Hashanah* teaches that six months earlier, on Rosh Hashanah, we were already freed from slave labor.[1]

The *Kli Yakar*, in explaining the four words connoting redemption, discusses four aspects of our slavery in Mitzrayim:

1. We were distanced from Hashem's presence, which is greater in Eretz Yisrael.
2. We were strangers in a foreign land.
3. We were slaves.
4. We were oppressed with backbreaking labor.

Similarly, Hashem redeemed us in four stages, each one correlating to one of the words of redemption:

1. He "took us out" from underneath the burden of the back-breaking labor.
2. He "saved us" from servitude.
3. He "redeemed us" from a foreign land.
4. And He "took us" as a people and returned His Divine presence.[2]

We drink four cups of wine on Pesach to commemorate these four stages.

Why is it so important that we recognize the various stages of the redemption?

On Purim there is a mitzvah to drink wine until we can no longer distinguish between "cursed be Haman and blessed be Mordechai." The *Mishnah Berurah* explains that Hashem performed two miracles on our behalf. The first miracle was the downfall of Haman, and the second was the elevation of Mordechai. "Before a person drinks wine, he surely thanks Hashem for both of these miracles. Chazal say that one should continue to praise Hashem with joy for these miracles until the point that one can no longer distinguish between the two of them."[3]

In order to appreciate the many things that Hashem does for us, it is necessary to break down the good aspects of life into all their various

---

1   *Rosh Hashanah* 11a.
2   *Kli Yakar, Shemos* 6:6.
3   *Mishnah Berurah* 695:4.

components. If we are healthy, it is not merely one blessing of health. Every one of our limbs and organs are functioning properly, and each one is miraculous. If we enjoy a *parnassah*, it is not merely that we "have what we need." We enjoy good and healthy food, we live in a home that shelters us from the outside, and we have obtained every single one of the objects that makes our life easier and more pleasurable. In truth, almost everything that we enjoy consists of multiple components for which we can be grateful.

Appreciate the multiple components of blessing in everything that you enjoy.

9b

WHAT LOOKS LIKE A BURDEN
MAY BE A BLESSING

בעל כרחם דישראל—משום משוי.

The Jewish People [carried the spoils of Egypt] against their own will. [They were not interested in taking the spoils] because it was too great a burden.

B'nei Yisrael didn't want the gold and silver from Mitzrayim because it would be a heavy burden. The journey out of Mitzrayim would not be easy. However, after tolerating the burden, it would leave them fabulously wealthy. Sometimes what looks to us like a burden is in reality a tremendous *berachah*.

The Gemara in *Sanhedrin* states that Yaakov redeemed Avraham from the pain of raising children.[1] *Rashi* explains that the difficulty involved in raising the twelve *shevatim* was originally intended to be Avraham's responsibility. When Yaakov ultimately raised the *shevatim*, he was, in a sense, relieving Avraham from that burden. *Tosafos* is troubled by *Rashi's* interpretation. "It is not painful to raise children. It is a joy! The Gemara teaches us that Oveid Edom was rewarded with many children."

---

1   *Sanhedrin* 19b.

Clearly, having many children is a blessing. *Tosafos* suggests that the pain of raising children that the Gemara refers to is not the difficulties of raising children in general, but rather the pain Yaakov experienced when Yosef was sold into slavery by his brothers.

The story is told that someone once blessed the Chafetz Chaim that he hoped the Chafetz Chaim would, in the future, walk barefoot while carrying heavy loads. Someone accompanying the Chafetz Chaim was aghast that anyone would dare curse the Chafetz Chaim. The Chafetz Chaim explained to him the meaning of the *berachah*. Kohanim in the Beis Hamikdash would walk barefoot because of the requirement that there not be an interruption (*chatzitzah*) between the Kohen's feet and the floor of the Beis Hamikdash. What could appear like a burden may actually be a beautiful opportunity that we have eagerly anticipated for centuries!

What seems like a burden may really be a blessing.

9b

THE MECHANICS OF ANXIETY

אהי-ה אשר אהי-ה. אמר לו הקדוש ברוך הוא למשה:
לך אמור להם לישראל: אני הייתי עמכם בשעבוד
זה ואני אהיה עמכם בשעבוד מלכיות. אמר לפניו:
רבונו של עולם! דיה לצרה בשעתה. אמר לו הקדוש
ברוך הוא: לך אמור להם אהי-ה שלחני אליכם.

[Moshe said to Hashem, "If the people ask, 'What is the name of the G-d who sent you,' what should I tell them?" Hashem replied,] "I will be, that I will be." [The Gemara explains that] Hashem was saying to Moshe, "Tell the Jewish People that I was with them throughout their servitude in Egypt and I will be with them through all of the future exiles that they will suffer." Moshe replied, "Master of the Universe, isn't it enough that they are currently experiencing suffering? Must I tell them of future exiles as well?" Hashem [accepted Moshe's argument and] replied, "Tell them that I have been with them in their suffering."

The risk-resource model of anxiety, formulated by Beck and Clark, postulates that anxiety is caused by over-evaluating risk and under-evaluating one's ability to cope.

Hashem tells Moshe to inform B'nei Yisrael that just as He helped them cope with slavery in Mitzrayim, so too He will help them cope with all of the future travails that may befall them. Moshe argues that it will be difficult for the people to hear that they will endure more hardships in the future. Hashem agrees and tells Moshe to inform the people that He who was with them throughout their suffering in Mitzrayim has sent him to take them out.

To deliver a prophecy of future suffering would mean to tell the people that the risk of future suffering is one hundred percent. Hashem agreed that this would be too difficult for them. Nonetheless, He wanted to imply that should any difficulties arise in the future, B'nei Yisrael could rely on Him just as He helped them cope with suffering in Mitzrayim. Hashem's goal was to comfort the people by minimizing their sense of risk and maximizing their sense of ability to cope.

A helpful method to alleviate anxiety is to evaluate anxiety-provoking thoughts by asking certain questions about the thought. "What is the worst that could happen, and if it happened how could I cope? What is the best that could happen? What is the most realistic outcome?"[1] Thinking about the best possible outcome and the most realistic outcome helps us realize that we were perhaps overestimating the risk. Thinking about how we could cope with the worst possible outcome helps us realize that we have the strength to manage future difficulties as they arise.

Avoid anxiety by assessing realistically both the likelihood of the negative event occurring and your ability to cope.

---

1   *CBT: Basics and Beyond*, p. 172.

9b

HUMILITY, GRATITUDE, AND LOVE OF MITZVOS

וְתִיקִין הָיוּ גּוֹמְרִין אוֹתָהּ עִם הָנֵץ הַחַמָּה.

"Vasikin" would recite the *Shema* right before sunrise.

Rashi defines *"vasikin"* as humble people who love to perform mitzvos. What is the connection between humility and the love of mitzvos?

A person who is humble values and respects others. It is a pleasure to do something for someone you respect and love. Thus, one who is humble will love to do favors for others. He will also savor the opportunity to give Hashem pleasure by performing His mitzvos.

The *Orchos Tzaddikim* writes: "The root of humility is thinking, at a time when one is at peace, [and has] health and wealth, that Hashem has given him so many favors that he did not do anything to deserve, as well as contemplating Hashem's greatness...and one thinks, 'All of the good that I can do is like a drop of water in the sea in comparison to what I owe to Hashem [for all of His favors to me].'"[1] This understand-

---

1   *Orchos Tzaddikim, Shaar Ha'anavah.*

ing leads to an intense desire to repay Hashem for all of His favors and a love for performing mitzvos.

Have the humility to value others, and enjoy reciprocating
the favors that they do for you.

9b

THE REWARD THAT AWAITS US

אמר ליה רבי אלעא לעולא: כי עיילת להתם שאיל
בשלמא דרב ברונא אחי במעמד כל החבורה, דאדם
גדול הוא ושמח במצות: זימנא חדא סמך גאולה
לתפלה ולא פסיק חוכא מפומיה כוליה יומא.

Rabbi Ila'ah said to Ulah, "When you travel to Eretz
Yisrael, greet my brother, Rav Bruna, in the presence
of the entire group, for he is a great man and rejoices
in mitzvos. One time, he recited the *berachah* of redemption right before saying *Shemoneh Esreh*, and he
was filled with laughter and joy for the entire day.

Rav Yitzchak Zilberstein relates the following story:

A young Jewish child living in a ghetto in Nazi Germany was
about to head out to cheder in the morning. He was thirsty,
and he asked his mother for something to drink. There was
nothing to drink in the home, and his mother told him to
knock on a door with a mezuzah and ask for something to
drink. The child found a home, knocked on the door, and while
crying, explained to the woman who answered that he was

very thirsty. She generously offered him something to drink, as well as several pieces of cake. Having quenched his thirst and gained additional strength, he went off to cheder with a smile.

Many years later, the woman, who was now elderly, was living in America. She grew ill and was told that she would need a surgery that was not covered by the insurance and would cost close to one million dollars. She had no choice but to go ahead with the surgery.

On the day of the surgery, her children gathered in the waiting room, anxious to hear from the doctor if it was successful. When the surgery was completed, the doctor emerged and told the children that everything went well and that their mother would be wheeled into the room shortly. The doctor then handed them a bill to cover the operation. They looked at it and were shocked to see the last line. After all of the calculations, the bill came out to over a million dollars, but right next to the price was written the words: "paid in full."

The doctor explained to the children that he was that boy in the ghetto and that their mother was the woman who had given him breakfast that morning. The operation for their mother was his way of repaying her for her kindness.[1]

Rav Zilberstein exclaims, "What did this woman truly do? She gave the child a drink and a few pieces of cake...And for this she was repaid with a million dollars...This can give us a glimpse of the reward for even the smallest of mitzvos that we perform in this world. In truth, 'No eyes but Yours, Hashem, have ever seen the great reward that You will give to those who await You.'"[2]

---

1   Rav Yitzchak Zilberstein, *Mitzvos B'Simchah*, vol. 2, introduction.
2   *Yeshayahu* 64:3.

The *Orchos Tzaddikim* writes that someone with *emunah* will serve Hashem with joy, "and even if it is very difficult for him, he will contemplate all of the good that the service of Hashem will bring him."[3]

Small actions can have immense value. Enjoy the mitzvos you do and the kindnesses that you perform. Their long-term effects can be immeasurably great.

---

3   *Orchos Tzaddikim, Shaar Hasimchah*, p. 85.

10a

THE HOLINESS WITHIN US

מה הקב"ה מלא כל העולם אף נשמה מלאה את
כל הגוף.

[David HaMelech, in *Tehillim*, uses the expression "My
soul shall bless" five times. There are five ways in which
Hashem and one's *neshamah* are similar, one of which is
that] just as Hashem fills the entire world, so too the
neshamah fills the entire body.

In describing the effect of Torah study on the world, the *Bach* describes how when one learns Torah for its own sake, the presence of Hashem descends to the world, and the entire world is filled with the light of Hashem's glory.[1] The world is elevated to a G-dly plane filled with spiritual light. When we learn that the *neshamah* fills the body just like Hashem fills the world, it doesn't merely mean that the *neshamah* "occupies the space" of the body. Our entire body is filled with the spiritual light of our *neshamah*. It is truly amazing how holy we are!

In the Rosh Hashanah davening, we declare, "It is fitting for the Holy One to be glorified by those who are holy." In the regular weekday

---

1   *Orach Chaim* 47:2.

davening, in the third *berachah* of *Shemoneh Esreh*—*Atah kadosh*, we say "Every day the holy will praise You forever." "The holy" is a reference to the Jewish People.[2]

How we view ourselves and the labels that we attribute to ourselves usually become self-fulfilling prophecies. An awareness of our great holiness can increase our positive feelings toward spirituality and motivate us to continue to invest efforts into our spiritual growth.

Be aware of the holiness within you.

---

2   *Pathway to Prayer.*

10b

INTERDEPENDENCE

אמר אביי ואיתימא רבי יצחק: הרוצה להנות–יהנה
כאלישע, ושאינו רוצה להנות אל יהנה כשמואל
הרמתי.

If one wants to benefit from others [by accepting gifts
or invitations], that is acceptable as we learn from
Elisha. If one does not want to benefit from others, that
is also acceptable as we learn from Shmuel.

Stephen Covey writes:

Life is, by nature, highly interdependent. To try to achieve
maximum effectiveness through independence is like trying
to play tennis with a golf club—the tool is not suited to the
reality. Interdependence is a far more mature, more advanced
concept. If I am physically interdependent, I am self-reliant
and capable, but I also realize that you and I working together
can accomplish far more than, even at my best, I could ac-
complish alone. If I am emotionally interdependent, I derive
a great sense of worth within myself, but I also recognize the
need for love, for giving, and for receiving love from others. If I

am intellectually interdependent, I realize that I need the best thinking of other people to join with my own.[1]

Sometimes it is uncomfortable to accept favors from others. At times, it is difficult to assert ourselves and make reasonable requests. When we notice these thoughts, it is helpful to think about all that we contribute and do for other people. Elisha, as one of the great *nevi'im* and leaders of the Jewish People, traveled to Shunem, presumably on important business on behalf of the entire community. His hostess offered him comfortable lodging, and he accepted the gift. The realization that he was doing so much for others presumably enabled him to feel comfortable accepting from others as well. The world is interdependent, and accepting favors enables us to continue to assist other people as well.

Sometimes it is difficult to accept favors. It can be easier if you recognize and appreciate how much you also do for others in our interdependent world.

---

1   *Seven Habits*, p. 58.

11a

WE CAN CONTROL OUR EMOTIONS BY CONTROLLING OUR THOUGHTS

אי משום טרדא, אפילו טבעה ספינתו בים נמי! וכי
תימא הכי נמי, אלמה אמר רבי אבא בר זבדא אמר
רב: אבל חייב בכל המצות האמורות בתורה, חוץ מן
התפילין...התם טריד טרדא דמצוה הכא טריד טרדא
דרשות.

[A *chassan* is exempt from reciting *Shema*. The Gemara suggests that perhaps the exemption is because he is preoccupied. To this, the Gemara responds:] "If it is because he is preoccupied, would one who lost one of his ships at sea also be exempt from *Shema*? And if you answer that indeed he would be exempt, then why does Rav teach that a mourner [who is certainly preoccupied] is obligated to fulfill all of the mitzvos except for tefillin?" The Gemara answers that a *chassan* is preoccupied by a mitzvah, whereas a mourner or one who lost his ships at sea is distracted by non-mitzvah matters.

One who experiences a loss—whether it be the passing of a relative or a great financial loss (such as one's ship sinking)—is not obligated or predetermined to experience emotional pain. The Gemara teaches in *Sukkah* that a mourner is obligated in the mitzvah of sukkah. Even though one who is uncomfortable in the sukkah is exempt from the mitzvah, that is only when it is sitting in the sukkah itself that is causing the discomfort. While the suffering and pain of a mourner is understood, the Gemara nonetheless says that from a halachic perspective, "He causes his own discomfort, and it is his responsibility to calm his mind."[1]

The point is that, to a large extent, our emotions *are* in our control. Robert Leahy writes:

> *The fundamental assumption guiding cognitive therapy is that the individual's interpretation of an event determines how he or she feels and behaves. Many people, in fact, are surprised to learn that their feelings are the result of how they think about an event, and that by modifying their interpretation of an event, they can have very different feelings...Often depressed, anxious, or angry individuals may claim that the "reason" they behaved a specific way or felt a specific way is that an event occurred...The implicit implication is that an event necessarily leads to a feeling...The cognitive therapist will want to examine further how the interpretation of the event led to the behavior or the emotion.*[2]

The *Sefer Hachinuch* explains the prohibition of jealousy. He writes, "We are forbidden from setting our thoughts to desire that which belongs to someone else."[3] Desire is an emotion. How are we to control our desires? The precise wording of the *Sefer Hachinuch* offers us guidance. If we do not focus our thoughts on desire, we will not experience

---

1   *Sukkah* 25b.
2   *Cognitive Therapy Techniques*, pp. 17, 19.
3   *Sefer Hachinuch* 417.

the emotion of desire. All emotions are outgrowths of our thoughts. We can control our thoughts, and thus, we *can* control our emotions.

You can control your emotions by controlling your thoughts. If you think positive thoughts, you will experience positive emotions.

11a

ACCEPT COMPLIMENTS

משל לאחד שאומרים לו זקנך מגודל, אמר להם:
יהיה כנגד המשחיתים.

This [a discussion relating to sitting or standing for *Shema*] is comparable to one who is told that he has a nicely grown beard, and responds by saying, "Since you complimented me on my beard, I will therefore shave it off."

The Gemara's parable illustrates how foolish it is to disqualify a compliment.

Dr. Burns lists various cognitive distortions (common errors in thinking). One of the distortions is where a person has the tendency to "transform neutral or even positive experiences into negative ones...An everyday example of this would be the way most of us have been conditioned to respond to compliments. When someone praises your appearance or your work, you might automatically tell yourself, "They're just being nice." With one swift blow, you mentally disqualify their compliment...If you constantly throw cold water on the good things that happen, no wonder life seems damp and chilly."[1]

It is not inappropriate or arrogant to notice and appreciate a compliment. On the contrary, it can give us the energy and motivation to continue to do good.

Don't disqualify compliments. Accept and enjoy them. Allow them to motivate you to continue to grow.

---

1   *Feeling Good*, p. 34.

11b

FIND A WIN/WIN COMPROMISE

תניא נמי הכי: אין אומרים אהבת עולם אלא אהבה
רבה. ורבנן אמרי: אהבת עולם.

[The Gemara relates a dispute about how to phrase
the beginning of the *berachah* that we say right before
Shema.] The Tanna Kama instructs one to say *Ahavah
Rabbah* ("with great love"), and the Rabbis instruct one
to say *Ahavas Olam* ("with eternal love").

Tosafos writes that since the Tanna Kama instructs one to say
Ahavah Rabbah, and the Rabbis instruct one to say *Ahavas Olam*, the
practice was established to say *Ahavah Rabbah* in the morning and
Ahavas Olam at night. *Tosafos Rabbeinu Peretz* adds that this practice
enables us to avoid the dispute and use the wording that satisfies all of
the opinions.

This is seemingly difficult. Rather than satisfying both of the opinions, we have guaranteed that according to each opinion we have erred
in at least one of the *tefillos*! What does *Tosafos Rabbeinu Peretz* mean
when he says that by following one opinion in the morning and the
other opinion in the afternoon, we have satisfied both opinions? We
haven't really satisfied either!

Perhaps the Rabbis believe that during both *tefillos* the *nusach* should be *Ahavas Olam*. Nonetheless, what is of primary importance to them is that *Ahavas Olam* be recited at least once a day. Similarly, the Tanna Kama believes that what is of the greatest importance is that *Ahavah Rabbah* be recited once a day. Each opinion is satisfied, as *Tosafos* teaches us, by the compromise that was enacted to say *Ahavah Rabbah* in the morning and *Ahavas Olam* at night. Perhaps each opinion would even acknowledge that there is an additional benefit to alternating the wording and incorporating the ideas contained in both formulations.

We see from here that compromise does not need to entail accepting only half of what one wants and conceding the rest. It is possible for a compromise to be ideal for both parties, and perhaps even better than what each of them originally sought.

Stephen Covey writes: "When you see only two alternatives—yours and the "wrong" one—you can look for a synergistic, third alternative. There's almost always a third alternative, and if you work with a Win/ Win philosophy and really seek to understand, you usually can find a solution that will be better for everyone concerned."[1]

When possible, don't just compromise. Find a third alternative that will benefit both you and the other in a way that exceeds even your original preference.

---

1   *Seven Habits*, p. 296.

11b

CONNECT WITH HASHEM THROUGH TORAH

ונהיה אנחנו וצאצאינו וצאצאי עמך בית ישראל
כלנו יודעי שמך ועוסקי תורתך.

[In the *berachah* that we make over learning Torah, we
say:] "May we and our children, and all of the children of
Your nation B'nei Yisrael, all of us, know Your name and
be involved in studying Your Torah."

In *Birkas HaTorah*, we ask Hashem, "May we and our children and
the children of Your nation, the People of Israel—all of us—know Your
Name and study Your Torah for its own sake." It appears that there
is a connection between studying Torah for its own sake and knowing Hashem.

The Chafetz Chaim explains that in order for our *neshamah* to connect
with Hashem, we require the Torah. Though our *neshamah* is spiritual,
since it is housed in a physical body, it is in some way "too physical"
to fully connect to the absolute spirituality of Hashem Himself. The
Torah that we learn is on a greater spiritual plane than our *neshamah*.
When it enters our *neshamah*, it serves as a connecting point between
the *neshamah* and Hashem. The Chafetz Chaim uses this idea to explain

the concept that "Hashem, the Torah, and the Jewish People are one." This is not to say that Hashem, the Torah, and the Jewish People are the same entity. It means instead that, in some respect, we are all connected to form one unit. It is the Torah that binds our *neshamos* to Hashem.

The enjoyment that we derive from learning Torah is enhanced with the recognition that the Torah we learn enters our *neshamos* and enables us to connect to Hashem in a deep spiritual way.

When you study Torah you are connecting with Hashem in a deep spiritual way. Enjoy!

12a

APPRECIATION
AND SATISFACTION

כל שלא אמר אמת ויציב שחרית ואמת ואמונה
ערבית—לא יצא ידי חובתו, שנאמר: להגיד בבקר
חסדך ואמונתך בלילות.

[In the morning, we say the *berachah* of *Emes V'Yatziv*,
which discusses the kindness that Hashem has done
for us in the past. In the evening, we say the *berachah*
of *Emes V'Emunah*, which speaks of our hope and faith
in the fulfillment of Hashem's promises for the future
redemption.] Anyone who has not recited *Emes V'Yatziv*
in the morning or *Emes V'Emunah* in the evening has
not fulfilled his obligation, as it states: "To relate Your
kindness in the morning and Your faithfulness at night."

In the morning, we recount the kindnesses that Hashem has done for
us in the past. In the evening, we express our faith in Hashem and our
trust that He will care for us in the future. The order here is significant.
It is essential that we first appreciate everything that we have, and only
after that we anticipate even better times in the future.

The Mishnah in *Pirkei Avos* lists being *samei'ach b'chelko* (being satisfied with what one has) as one of the necessary traits for acquiring Torah knowledge. To be satisfied with what one has includes not only physical possessions but also the situation in which one finds oneself. *Emes V'Yatziv* describes our appreciation that we are no longer slaves in Mitzrayim. *Emes V'Emunah* primarily describes our anticipation that Hashem will free us from evil rulers who have ruled over us throughout the *galus*. We first appreciate our freedom and only afterward we speak about a time of independence from cruel monarchs.

Another aspect of *simchah b'chelko* is to be satisfied with one's spiritual accomplishments.[1] Despite your ambitions to continue to grow, you must also enjoy the growth that you have already achieved.

In material matters, obtaining one's desire usually doesn't lead to prolonged happiness. The midrash says, "One who has one hundred wants two hundred, and one who has two hundred wants four hundred."[2] The *pasuk* teaches us that one who loves money will not be satisfied by money. What is surprising is that the Gemara states that this applies to mitzvos as well. One who loves mitzvos will not be satisfied by mitzvos.[3] What does this mean? The Gemara explains that a person who loves mitzvos will always be looking for the opportunity to do more mitzvos and continuously grow in *avodas Hashem*. Does this mean that one whose ambitions are in spiritual matters will also never find satisfaction and happiness? Will he always feel that he is lacking a greater level of serving Hashem?

Rav Chaim Friedlander explains that there is a fundamental difference between striving for material possessions and striving for spiritual growth:[4]

- In material matters, shortly after one attains his desire, he notices that it has not granted him the happiness that he expected it would. Rather than concluding that physical items can't provide

---

1   See *Ruach Chaim*.
2   *Midrash Rabbah, Koheles* 1:34.
3   *Makkos* 10a.
4   Rabbi Chaim Friedlander, *Sifsei Chaim, Middos V'Avodas Hashem*.

happiness, he instead mistakenly concludes that it is just that he needs an additional item to procure that happiness. The cycle continues, and the happiness is never attained (in a long-lived, significant manner).

- When one strives for spiritual growth, the cycle is very different. After you attain your goal, you experience a true sense of happiness and satisfaction over your accomplishment and your newfound closeness to Hashem. The joy you experience motivates you to continue to grow. The desire for reaching the next level is not out of an attempt to capture an elusive happiness that you never experienced. Instead, it is an effort to replicate the happiness that you *have* experienced.

(If spiritual growth doesn't grant a person happiness, there is reason for concern that perhaps his motivation for spiritual growth is not truly to come closer to Hashem. For example, one who does a mitzvah in order to be honored or recognized may not experience happiness after fulfilling the mitzvah if he did not achieve recognition. This is because his spiritual pursuit is actually a materialistic pursuit. Similarly, if one does mitzvos merely out of habit, he may not experience joy from the mitzvos simply because he does not contemplate the meaning of the accomplishment.)

Appreciate what you do have before seeking more.
Appreciate your spiritual accomplishments.

12a

THE BLESSING OF SLEEP

כל שלא אמר אמת ויציב שחרית ואמת ואמונה
ערבית—לא יצא ידי חובתו, שנאמר: להגיד בבקר
חסדך ואמונתך בלילות.

[*Tosafos* explains that *Emes V'Emunah* is about our trust
in Hashem that he will restore our *neshamos*, and that
we will wake up refreshed the next day. This is what the
pasuk refers to when it says, "*rabbah emunasecha—*
great is your faithfulness."]

The *berachah* of sleep and everything that it accomplishes for a
person is a very significant *chessed* that Hashem has given humanity.
Dr. James Maas, previous chairman of the psychology department at
Cornell University, writes:[1]

*The process of sleep, if given adequate time and the proper envi-
ronment, provides tremendous power. It restores, rejuvenates,
and energizes the body and brain. The third of your life that
you should spend sleeping has profound effects on the other
two-thirds of your life in terms of alertness, energy, mood,*

---

1   Dr. James Maas, *Power Sleep*, p. 6.

body weight, perception, memory, thinking, reaction time, productivity, performance, communication skills, creativity, safety, and good health."

Hashem gave us the berachah of sleep to refresh us for the next day. Take advantage and get adequate sleep.

12b

IT'S EASY TO REPENT AND BEGIN ANEW

ואמר רבה בר חיננא סבא משמיה דרב: כל העושה
דבר עבירה ומתבייש בו—מוחלין לו על כל עונותיו.

When one is embarrassed over a sin that they have
committed, they are forgiven for all of their sins.

David HaMelech says, "For with You is forgiveness, so that you will be feared."[1] How does Hashem's ability to forgive increase our fear of Heaven? Seemingly, it would allay our fears with the knowledge that sin is not so catastrophic, as we can always attain forgiveness.

The *Ibn Ezra* explains that David HaMelech was saying, "When You forgive my sin, other sinners will hear. They will repent and abandon their sins. If, however, You don't forgive me, they will not fear You and they will continue in their ways."

The knowledge that all is not already lost, that Hashem forgives, and that we have the potential to start anew is what motivates us to return to Hashem.

---

1   *Tehillim* 130:4.

Our Gemara teaches us that if we are embarrassed over one sin that we have committed, we are forgiven for all of our sins. According to *Rashi's* interpretation—that Shaul was embarrassed in front of Shmuel—we see that one attains forgiveness even if one is merely embarrassed before another person (and not embarrassed before Hashem Himself).

It is not exceedingly difficult to earn forgiveness and to begin with a new clean slate. The Gemara in *Shabbos* teaches that if one properly observes Shabbos, even if he has worshipped idols he is forgiven.[2] Chazal instituted that one who steals a beam and builds it into a house need only repay the value of the beam. He need not take down the house to return the beam. Chazal understood that the greatest deterrence to repentance is the perception that it is exceptionally difficult. With the recognition that it is easy to begin with a fresh start, it is not nearly as challenging.

Repentance is not exceedingly difficult. Don't be overwhelmed.

---

2   *Shabbos* 118b.

12b

MAKE DECISIONS FROM THE BEGINNING

אחרי לבבכם—זו מינות, וכן הוא אומר: אמר נבל
בלבו אין אלקים.

[When the Torah warns us,] "Do not stray after your hearts," it is referring to heresy, as the *pasuk* says, "Naval said in his heart, 'There is no G-d.'"

The *Biur Halachah* in *siman* 1 quotes our Gemara, and adds that any foreign ideology that runs counter to the Torah is also considered heresy.

The Gemara understands that the *pasuk* that instructs us not to "stray after your hearts" is referring to heresy because of a derivation from the *pasuk* that says "Naval said in his heart, 'There is no G-d.'" Denying G-d is, of course, heresy. How can the *Biur Halachah* extrapolate from a blatant denial of G-d to a seemingly less severe infraction of accepting a foreign ideology?

Perhaps we can answer this question based on an idea found in the *sefer Bilvavi Mishkan Evneh*. There, it suggests the following advice for someone who is struggling to make an important decision. He recommends thinking about the situation from the very beginning. Your thoughts should begin with the fact that Hashem created the world.

The purpose of Creation was, as the *Mesilas Yesharim* explains, to give mankind the greatest possible pleasure attainable. This pleasure can only be spiritual, and it is primarily experienced in the World to Come. In order to earn this pleasure of the World to Come, each person was given a specific mission to accomplish. That mission includes fulfilling the mitzvos and accomplishing their mission in life. With this background, you can then proceed to think about a particular situation and a particular decision.

A person who adopts a foreign ideology, and especially someone who makes life decisions based on a foreign ideology, is in essence unable to make the proper choice because of a flaw in the decision-making process. If one believes that Hashem created the world in order to bestow good upon mankind, and that through serving Hashem we earn the ultimate spiritual reward, it is impossible to adopt a foreign ideology. It is not the foreign ideology itself that is heresy but rather that it is symptomatic of underlying heretical beliefs.

This idea of the *Bilvavi Mishkan Evneh* is similar to one of the seven habits described by Stephen Covey, who writes:

> *The most fundamental application of "begin with the end in mind" is to begin today with the image, picture, or paradigm of the end of your life as your frame of reference or the criterion by which everything else is examined. Each part of your life—today's behavior, tomorrow's behavior, next week's behavior, next month's behavior—can be examined in the context of the whole, of what really matters most to you. By keeping that end clearly in mind, you can make certain that whatever you do on any particular day does not violate the criteria you have defined as supremely important, and that each day of your life contributes in a meaningful way to the vision you have of your life as a whole. To begin with the end in mind means to start with a clear understanding of your destination. It means to know where you're going so that you better understand where*

you are now and so that the steps you take are always in the right direction.[1]

Begin with the end in mind, and determine what end to pursue by understanding the world and its purpose from the beginning.

---

1   *Seven Habits*, p. 105.

12b

COMPARATIVELY GOOD

הנה ימים באים נאם ה' ולא יאמרו עוד חי ה' אשר
העלה את בני ישראל מארץ מצרים, כי אם חי ה'
אשר העלה ואשר הביא את זרע בית ישראל מארץ
צפונה ומכל הארצות אשר הדחתים שם!

Days are coming—the word of Hashem—when people will
no longer say, "As Hashem lives, Who brought the People
of Israel up from the land of Egypt," but rather, "As
Hashem lives, Who brought up and brought the children
of the People of Israel from the land of the North and
from all the lands where He had dispersed them."

The Gemara explains that the future redemption will be so significant that it will make the redemption from Mitzrayim pale in comparison. The Gemara compares this to a person who was miraculously saved
from a wolf. He would frequently relate the story of how he was saved.
Later, he was miraculously saved from a lion. From that time on, he
would no longer speak about the wolf. Instead, he told everyone about
the miracle of being saved from the lion. When he was miraculously
saved from a dangerous snake, he forgot about the first two episodes

and would only relate the newest greater miracle of being saved from the vicious snake.

Something that today seems like an inconquerable hurdle may later prove to be of much lesser difficulty than other challenges that may arise in the future. Knowing that a situation is more manageable than it could otherwise have been can make it is easier to tolerate the difficulty.

The story is told of the man who felt overcrowded in his small hut. The Rabbi of his town advised him to bring several animals into his home for a week. When the week came to an end, the man was so relieved to remove the animals from his home that, in contrast to the previous week, he felt that his home was quite spacious.

The Gemara in *Nedarim* relates that when Rabbi Akiva married, he was so poor that he and his wife slept on beds of straw. Eliyahu the Prophet came to his door appearing like a beggar, and told Rabbi Akiva that his wife had just given birth and that he didn't have any straw with which to make a bed for her. Rabbi Akiva turned to his wife and said, "You see, there are even those who do not have straw!"[1] The *Ran* explains that Eliyahu intended to comfort Rabbi Akiva and his wife by showing them that there were those who were even more unfortunate than themselves.

While it's usually not worthwhile to make things more difficult for ourselves, it is worthwhile to think about how things could be more difficult. We can then come to recognize our ability to manage in the current situation.

In difficult situations, it can sometimes be helpful to contemplate how the situation could be even more challenging.

---

1   *Nedarim* 50a.

13a

START WITH YOURSELF

אברם הוא אברהם, בתחלה נעשה אב לארם, ולבסוף
נעשה אב לכל העולם כולו.

Avram is the same person as Avraham. Originally, he
was a "father" to the people of Aram, and ultimately, he
became a "father" to the entire world.

Rav Yisrael Salanter reportedly made the following observation: He said that when he was very young, he wanted to change the world. As he grew older, he recognized that such an accomplishment was not possible. Instead, his ambition was to change his town. When he recognized that even that was not possible, he decided to change his family. Eventually he realized that the only person he could change was himself. As we know, Rav Yisrael Salanter not only succeeded in improving himself. His self-improvement then had a ripple effect on all of his surroundings. Ultimately, he inspired the entire world to become a better place as well.

Rav Mordechai Willig notes that even when Hashem changes Avram's name to Avraham, the "*reish*" of Avram remains in his name. "Avram" is an acronym for Avraham being a "father" to Aram. "Avraham" is an acronym for Avraham being a father to all of the multitudes of nations

117

(*av hamon goyim*). Why does the *reish* remain if it is not necessary for the latter acronym? Rav Willig answers that in order for you to have a positive effect on all of humanity, you must begin by having a positive effect on those who are closest to you. It is because Avraham was an *av l'Aram* that he was able to be an *av hamon goyim*.

Stephen Covey discusses the transition in personal growth literature from "Character Ethic" to "Personality Ethic." Covey describes how he surveyed two hundred years of writing on the topic of success, beginning in 1776. What he noticed was that "the success literature of the past fifty years was superficial...Success became more a function of personality, of public image, of attitudes and behaviors, skills and techniques, that lubricate the processes of human interaction...In stark contrast, almost all the literature in the first 150 years or so focused on what could be called the Character Ethic as the foundation of success—things like integrity, humility, fidelity, temperance, courage, justice, patience, industry, simplicity, modesty, and the golden rule."[1]

From a Torah perspective, it is the Character Ethic which is the foundation of success. It is only by improving ourselves that we are then able to successfully help others improve as well.

In order to be successful in positively influencing other people, you must begin with the character ethic of developing yourself.

---

1   *Seven Habits*, p. 26.

PEREK 2

13a

GIVE YOURSELF CREDIT

שמע מינה: מצות צריכות כוונה! מאי אם כוון לבו—
לקרות. לקרות? והא קא קרי! בקורא להגיה.

[The Mishnah rules that one who focuses while reading
the verses of *Shema* fulfills his obligation. The Gemara
suggests that we should] derive from here that mitzvos
require intent! [No, perhaps the Mishnah means to say,]
what is "focus one's heart?"–to read it. Read it? He's
reading it! [No,] he's merely reading it to check it over.

The Gemara defends the opinion that one can fulfill a mitzvah even
if he didn't have the intent to do so at the time of the performance of
the mitzvah. (This is a matter of dispute in the Gemara in *Masechta
Rosh Hashanah*. We follow the opinion that Biblical commandments do
require intent.)

Mitzvos d'Oraisa require intent to fulfill the mitzvah. Nevertheless,
there are still situations in which mitzvos performed without intent
can have great significance

Rashi in *Parashas Vayikra*[1] quotes the *Toras Kohanim* that discusses the reward that one receives for accidentally fulfilling a mitzvah. If one is harvesting one's field and forgets a bundle of sheaves in the field, one is required to leave the bundle behind for the poor. The Torah states that one who does so receives *berachah* from Hakadosh Baruch Hu. Rabbi Elazar ben Azaryah derives from there that if a coin fell out of your pocket and it is found by a poor man who uses it to support himself, you will receive Hashem's *berachah*. We see from here that we are rewarded for mitzvos fulfilled without intent.

There is more: We are even rewarded for mitzvos that we fulfill out of our own self-interest. The *pasuk* in *Shir Hashirim* says, "His palate is sweet and He is entirely a delight."[2] *Rashi* explains, "'His palate is sweet' [i.e., His words are sweet]. The Torah says that one may not cut himself and that Hashem will reward those who abide by this commandment. Is there anything sweeter than this—don't injure yourself and you will be rewarded." The mitzvos of the Torah are all for our benefit. Many of the mitzvos are self-evident, and we would observe them even if we were not commanded. Despite the fact that our intent in fulfilling these mitzvos is partially for our own benefit, Hashem grants us reward.

The *Chovos Halevavos* describes five categories of people who do favors for others. After elaborating on the categories, he writes, "Any person who does a favor for another intends, to some degree, to benefit himself as well, whether it be in this world or the next...Nevertheless, the recipient must thank his benefactor, love him, [and] attempt, in some way, to repay the favor."[3]

Sometimes we perform mitzvos and we don't give ourselves enough credit. We think, "I didn't do it with the ideal intentions," "Everyone does this," "Anyone would do this," "I hardly did anything," etc. We discount the value of our *avodah*, and as a result, we lose out on the encouragement that we could derive from a proper appreciation of the good that we do.

---

1   *Vayikra* 5:17.
2   *Shir Hashirim* 5:16.
3   *Shaar Avodas Elokim*, introduction.

"Discounting the positive" is one of the cognitive distortions that contribute to feeling down. Dr. Burns writes:

> *An everyday example of this would be the way most of us have been conditioned to respond to compliments…"They're just being nice." With one swift blow you mentally disqualify their compliment…Disqualifying the positive is one of the most destructive forms of cognitive distortion. You're like a scientist intent on finding evidence to support some pet hypothesis. The hypothesis that dominates your depressive thinking is usually some version of "I'm second rate." Whenever you have a negative experience, you dwell on it and conclude, "That proves what I've known all along." In contrast, when you have a positive experience, you tell yourself, "That was a fluke. It doesn't count." The price you pay for this tendency is intense misery and an inability to appreciate the good things that happen.*[4]

The Torah view is that no good is to ever be discounted. Every good act has immense value, even if it is not done with the most ideal intentions and even if it seems minor or insignificant. Give yourself credit for all the good that you do and enjoy the encouragement that you can derive from it!

Don't discount the good that you do just because it isn't perfect. Feel good about it and you will be motivated to continue growing.

---

4   *Feeling Good*, p. 35.

13a

WORDS ARE POWERFUL

למימרא דסבר רבי דכל התורה כולה בכל לשון
נאמרה.

[Rebbi *paskens* that the *Shema* must be recited in
Hebrew. The words, "And they (the words of the *Shema*)
will be" teach us that the words must remain in their
current state, i.e., Hebrew. The Gemara makes the following inference:] It appears from here that Rebbi holds
that the rest of the Torah, for which there is no similar
derashah, may be read in any language.

Tosafos explains that certain *parshiyos* that must be recited
may be recited in any language because when Hashem gave us the
Ten Commandments at Har Sinai, each of Hashem's words split into
all of the seventy languages. We can learn from here that the words
of every language are special and contain a degree of *kedushah*. While
lashon ha'kodesh is of course holier and of a higher nature, there is some
spiritual power to words of any language.

Rav Avraham Pam, the Rosh Yeshiva of Torah Vodaas, taught that it
is very important to choose one's words carefully. "In one *shmuess*, Rav
Pam added a new word to the list of those that should not pass our

lips: "whatchamicallit." He said, "What kind of word is this?" Later, a *talmid* asked, "What's wrong with 'watchamicallit'?" Rav Pam replied, "Don't you understand? How can you speak without thinking? If you don't know what you want to say, then think. But what kind of a word is 'watchamicallit'?"[1]

Words are powerful regardless of what language one is speaking. It is important to choose our words carefully.

Your words are powerful and important. Choose them carefully.

---

1   *The Life and Ideals of Rav Avraham Yaakov Hakohen Pam*, p. 301.

13b

ENJOY AND VALUE THE PROCESS

תניא סומכוס אומר כל המאריך באחד מאריכין לו
ימיו ושנותיו. אמר רב אחא בר יעקב ובדלי"ת. אמר
רב אשי ובלבד שלא יחטוף בחי"ת.

Sumchus says, "Anyone who extends the word *echad*
in *Shema* will be blessed with longevity." Rav Achah bar
Yaakov says, "He should extend the *dalet*." Rav Ashi says
"Provided that he doesn't cut the *ches* short."

Extending the *dalet* of the word *echad* in *Shema* is so significant that, in its merit, the Gemara promises long life. But don't rush
through the *ches* in your eagerness to extend the *dalet*. If the *ches* is not
enunciated properly, there is no value to extending the *dalet*.

There are many projects that we pursue in life where the final result is
so valuable that we're tempted to rush through the process. As a result,
we sometimes end up losing out on the valuable result. It is essential to
subscribe value to the process as well and to understand the significance
of all of the building blocks along the way.

The *berachos* of *Parashas Bechukosai* are introduced with the condi-
tion that "if you will abide by My decrees..." *Rashi*, quoting Chazal,
explains that this refers to involvement in studying Torah. How did

Chazal know this? The simple explanation is that the *pasuk* goes on to say that we must observe the mitzvos, so the earlier part of the *pasuk* must be referring to something else, namely the study of Torah. Rav Moshe Rosemarin adds an additional explanation: The word that the Torah uses for "following" Hashem's decrees is *"teileichu,"* which literally means "to walk." It must refer to a mitzvah where the primary objective is the process itself rather than the end result. This is how Chazal knew that the words refer to studying Torah, which is a mitzvah where the process of study is an end unto itself.

John Maxwell writes:

> *Eugene Griessman, author of The Path to High Achievement, says that most grand masters of chess learn and re-learn chess moves, gambits, and combinations over a period of fifteen years before they win their first world title. That's a fifth of most people's lives. If you're going to spend that much time learning something, then you had better learn to like it. If the destination appeals to you, but you cannot enjoy the journey it takes to get there, you would be wise to reexamine your priorities to make sure you have them right.[1]*

Later, Maxwell writes, "If we desire to improve a little every day and plan it that way, then we can make great progress over the long haul."[2]

Recognize that the building blocks are important components of the end result, and that frequently the process itself is inherently valuable. Enjoy the entire process! Think about the benefits of what you are doing in the moment!

Value the process. Don't wait until you've accomplished something before you enjoy it. Enjoy the entire process along the way.

---

1   John Maxwell, *Make Today Count*, p. 123.
2   Ibid., p. 126.

13b

PRESERVE YOUR PEACE OF MIND

על לבבך בעמידה.

[The beginning of the *Shema*, up until the words] *"al levavecha,"* must be recited while one is stationary.

Tosafos explains that one does not have as much peace of mind while walking, and it is therefore difficult to concentrate.

Whenever we try to multitask, it is hard to devote all of our energies to the primary matter at hand. Rav Chaim Friedlander explains that the secret to peace of mind is the ability to focus on only the matter at hand.[1] When you are distracted by thinking about the past or busy planning for the future, it is difficult to be present in the moment. Too many things are pulling for your attention and they destroy your peace of mind. Peace of mind requires pausing all of that and focusing on the present.

Walking detracts from our ability to concentrate in another way as well. The exertion can drain a person's energy and make it more difficult to concentrate. We find this concern in other areas of halachah and *avodas ha'middos* as well. The Gemara in *Sukkah* teaches that one

---

1   *Sifsei Chaim, Middos V'Avodas Hashem*, vol. 2, p. 17.

may not travel more than three *parsah* on Erev Shabbos.[2] One opinion in the Gemara is that this is only a prohibition if one is traveling to return to their own house. *Rashi* explains the concern—that his family is not expecting him to return home before Shabbos, and they did not prepare food for his Shabbos meal. When he returns and sees that he doesn't have a Shabbos meal, he may become angry with his family. The *Mishnah Berurah* quotes the *Bach*, who is lenient to allow one who travels in a wagon to travel even later in the day (not only that he may travel a further distance because the wagon travels faster, but that he may even remain on the road until much later in the day).[3] The *Piskei Teshuvos* explains that this is because one who walks will arrive exhausted and be unable to muster up the energy to prepare for Shabbos in the remaining time that he has on Friday afternoon. One who rides in a wagon, even if he arrives later, will use the remaining time to prepare a Shabbos meal.[4] Perhaps we can suggest the same distinction within *Rashi's* explanation as well: One who arrives exhausted will be more likely to grow angry with his family for not having prepared a meal for him.

Dr. Jerry Deffenbacher writes: "Anger is tremendously influenced by your immediate mental, emotional, and physical state. If you're feeling well and in a calm, relaxed state of mind, you are much less likely to become angry. The positive state of affairs seems to buffer angry feelings. Other conditions can lower the threshold for anger."[5]

When one is drained from traveling, it is difficult to concentrate on *tefillah*, *k'rias Shema*, and to have the peace of mind necessary for interacting positively with others.

What can we do to make traveling less stressful?

Richard Carlson writes:

> *Where do you get the most uptight? If you're like most people,*
> *driving in traffic is probably high on your list...Try to see your*
> *driving not only as a way of getting you somewhere, but as*

---

2   *Sukkah* 44b.
3   *Mishnah Berurah* 249:1.
4   *Piskei Teshuvos* 249, footnote 5.
5   Dr. Deffenbacher, *Overcoming Situational and General Anger*, p. 4.

a chance to breathe and to reflect. Rather than tensing your muscles, see if you can relax them instead...By the time I reach my destination, I feel more relaxed than I did before getting into the car. During the course of your lifetime, you're probably going to spend a great deal of time driving. You can spend those moments being frustrated, or you can use them wisely. If you do the latter, you'll be a more relaxed person.[6]

Maintain your peace of mind by focusing on one thing at a time. Your peace of mind is essential and will help you avoid negative emotional reactions such as anger. Commuting can be stressful. Try to use the time productively and avoid the stress.

---

6   Richard Carlson, *Don't Sweat the Small Stuff*, p. 141.

14a

HAVE THE PATIENCE
TO UNDERSTAND

ימים שהיחיד גומר בהן את ההלל...ימים שאין היחיד
גומר בהן את ההלל.

[There are days] that the individual completes the *Hallel*,
and [there are] days that the individual does not [but
says half-*Hallel*].

The Gemara implies that there are certain days when *Hallel* is not
completed but there is nonetheless an obligation to say half-*Hallel*.
Tosafos comments that this is not so. On days when the full *Hallel*
is not recited, it is only a custom to recite half-*Hallel*. *Tosafos* quotes
two proofs to support this assertion, one of which is a story from the
Gemara in *Masechta Taanis*.

The Gemara relates that Rav traveled to Bavel and entered one of the
shuls on Rosh Chodesh. He saw that they were reciting *Hallel*. Because
there is no obligation to recite *Hallel* on Rosh Chodesh (though we have
the custom to recite it), he was going to prevent them from continuing.
When he saw that they skipped paragraphs (they were reciting half-
Hallel), he said, "They are merely following their familial custom."

Tosafos explains that on days when *Hallel* is obligatory and the full *Hallel* is recited, the practice was to begin *Hallel* with the *berachah*, "...to complete the *Hallel*." On days when only half-*Hallel* was recited, the practice was to recite the *berachah*, "...to read the *Hallel*." *Tosafos* points out that presumably the people of Bavel said the *berachah*, "...to read the *Hallel*" since they didn't intend to complete the full *Hallel*. If so, asks *Tosafos*, why didn't Rav recognize immediately upon hearing the *berachah* that the people merely intended to recite half-*Hallel* as was their custom? *Tosafos* answers that, in reality, either *berachah* can be recited, regardless of whether one is saying the full *Hallel* or half-*Hallel*. The custom developed to say "to complete" when saying the full *Hallel* and "to read" when saying half-*Hallel* only to serve as a reminder to the people which *Hallel* they were about to say. When Rav entered the shul, he heard them saying the *berachah*, "to complete," and he therefore thought that they would say the full *Hallel*. He only recognized that they were merely saying half-*Hallel*, as was their custom, when they began to skip paragraphs.

There is a lesson that we can learn from here about Rav's humility and his willingness to wait and listen. Rav was one of the greatest Torah scholars of the generation. He entered a shul and heard the *berachah* that is usually recited over the obligatory full-*Hallel*, which would have been a mistake on Rosh Chodesh. Rav remained silent. He didn't jump to the conclusion that a mistake was made. He was aware that he was missing context and information, and he continued to wait for several paragraphs until he discovered that, in fact, no mistake was made.

Stephen Covey's fifth "Habit" of his *Seven Habits of Highly Effective People* is, "Seek first to understand, then to be understood." He relates the following example:

> Suppose you've been having trouble with your eyes, and you decide to go to an optometrist for help. After briefly listening to your complaint, he takes off his glasses and hands them to you. "Put these on," he says. "I've worn this pair of glasses for ten years now, and they've really helped me. I have an extra pair at home; you can wear these." So you put them on, but it only

makes the problem worse. "This is terrible!" you exclaim. "I can't see a thing!" "Well, what's wrong?" he asks. "They work great for me. Try harder"...What are the chances you'd go back to that optometrist the next time you needed help? Not very good, I would imagine. You don't have much confidence in someone who doesn't diagnose before he or she prescribes. But how often do we diagnose before we prescribe in communication?...

Empathic listening gets inside another person's frame of reference. You look out through it, you see the world the way they see the world, you understand their paradigm, you understand how they feel...Now, there are people who protest that empathic listening takes too much time. It may take a little more time initially but it saves so much time downstream. The most efficient thing you can do if you're a doctor and want to prescribe a wise treatment is to make an accurate diagnosis. You can't say, "I'm in too much of a hurry. I don't have time to make a diagnosis. Just take this treatment."[1]

Be patient and seek to understand. Listen empathically.

---

1   *Seven Habits*, p. 248.

14a

GREET WITH A SMILE

—אמר רב: כל הנותן שלום לחבירו קודם שיתפלל
כאילו עשאו במה.

Rav says, "One who greets his friend before davening is
considered as if he built a forbidden *mizbei'ach*."

To greet someone before davening in the morning is compared to building an illegitimate *mizbei'ach*. It is giving a human being the respect that is really due to Hashem. We see from here the extent to which a greeting is considered a sign of respect. Greeting another person is not considered to be a mere social norm. It is a way of recognizing and acknowledging the person as someone who is inherently worthy of respect.

The Mishnah in *Pirkei Avos* teaches that we should greet one another "*b'sever panim yafos.*"[1] What exactly do these three words mean? Rav Avigdor Miller explains that "*sever*" means "with thought" (from the same root as the word "*sevara*"). When greeting someone, we show them our *panim*, our face. But it is not just a blank stare; it is a face with an expression that demonstrates that we are thinking and that we are

---

1   *Avos* 1:15.

focused on them. The type of facial expression that we are meant to have is a pleasant one—a *"sever panim yafos."*

Dale Carnegie writes:

> *Actions speak louder than words, and a smile says, "I like you. You make me happy. I am glad to see you…An insincere grin? No. That doesn't fool anybody. We know it is mechanical, and we resent it. I am talking about a real smile, a heartwarming smile, a smile that comes from within…You must have a good time meeting people if you expect them to have a good time meeting you…Your smile is a messenger of your good will. Your smile brightens the lives of all who see it. To someone who has seen a dozen people frown, scowl, or turn their faces away, your smile is like the sun breaking through the clouds. Especially when that someone is under pressure from his bosses, his customers, his teachers, or parents, or children, a smile can help him realize that all is not hopeless—that there is joy in the world.[2]*

Greet people with a sincere smile that shows that you truly are happy to see them.

---

2   *Win Friends and Influence People*, p. 63.

14a

THE PLEASURE OF TORAH

כל המשביע עצמו מדברי תורה ולן—אין מבשרין
אותו בשורות רעות.

One who satisfies himself with words of Torah before
going to sleep is guaranteed that he will not receive bad
tidings.

One of the Chafetz Chaim's *talmidim* once related having seen the Chafetz Chaim complete a *Tosafos* and smack his lips as if he had just enjoyed a juicy piece of steak.

When the Gemara refers to "satisfying oneself with Torah," the same verb ("*savei'a*") is used, as if one had satisfied themselves with a sumptuous meal. This imagery is used repeatedly in Chazal.

The Gemara in *Bava Basra* speaks of a *talmid* who was punished for speaking with chutzpah about the righteous scholar Abaye. He was a *talmid* of Rava, and he exclaimed, "Rather than eating lean meat at the house of Abaye, come eat good, fatty, juicy meat at the house of Rava."[1]

---

1   *Bava Basra* 22a.

The *Rama* uses a similar comparison, and writes that one should only begin to study the mystical teachings of the Torah after having already filled oneself with the meat and wine of Torah.[2]

The *pasuk* in *Shir Hashirim* says, "He brought me to the house of wine."[3] *Rashi* explains that this is a reference to the *Ohel Moed* where the details and explanations of the Torah were given to the Jewish People.

On Shabbos morning, we recite the *pasuk* from *Tehillim* where David HaMelech exclaims that the Torah is more desirable than gold and sweeter than honey. Because most of us don't do business in gold and don't consume plain honey, the power of the analogy is lost. In order to properly appreciate this comparison, it can be helpful to translate gold and honey into their modern-day equivalents. David HaMelech is telling us that Torah is more precious than a multimillion-dollar bank account or the winning lottery ticket, and it is sweeter than our favorite dessert—whether it be ice cream cake, chocolate chip cookies, or brownies. Imagine the pleasure we would have if we were given any of these delicious desserts or financial treasures. The pleasure of Torah is so much greater!

Studying Torah is a pleasure. The Torah is so precious and so delicious.

---

2 *Rama, Yoreh Deah* 246:4.
3 *Shir Hashirim* 2:4.

14b

COMPLETE WHAT YOU START

לא יתחיל, ואם התחיל—גומר.

While it is not necessary to recite [the third paragraph
of the *Shema* in the evening], if one began reciting it,
one must complete it. [This is one opinion, which is not
accepted halachically.]

The importance of completing the projects that we begin is found in
numerous sources in Chazal.

On the second day of creation, *Rashi* observes that the Torah does not
say, "Hashem saw that it was good." *Rashi* explains that on the second
day, Hashem created the sky to separate between the heavenly and
earthly waters. On the third day, Hashem separated the waters of the
oceans and the dry land. Since the task involving the waters was not yet
complete on the second day, Hashem could not say that "it was good."

The Gemara in *Sotah* asks the following question: One *pasuk* says that
Moshe took the bones of Yosef in order to carry them up to Eretz Yisrael
for burial. Another *pasuk* says that, in fact, it was B'nei Yisrael who carried Yosef's bones to Eretz Yisrael for burial. The Gemara resolves this
contradiction by saying that if one person does not complete the task
and another comes and finishes it, the one who finishes it is credited

with having accomplished the entire task. Since the B'nei Yisrael completed the burial, they are credited with performing the entire mitzvah.[1]

The Gemara in *Kesubos* lists certain types of people who should not receive rabbinic ordination. One type of person listed is *"chamisin."*[2] *Rashi* explains that this refers to people who only provide one fifth of the explanation for the halachah being studied. The *Aruch* understands that it refers to someone who only studies one fifth of the *masechta*.

This is not to say that we should *always* finish everything that we start. If we realize that it isn't worthwhile to continue with a project, we shouldn't continue just because we have already invested so much into it. Robert Leahy writes:

> *Rational decision-making focuses on future cost-benefit ratios—that is on future utility...However, many people will focus on a cost they have already incurred for a behavior...We may think that we need to prove that we are right about making our decisions and that giving up a sunk cost will prove that we made a mistake. We fear regret, so we ride a loser in the hope that things will improve. We may be concerned with how bad we will feel in giving up the sunk cost...We may not anticipate the positive opportunities that might follow once we have abandoned a sunk cost...We may be overly concerned with how others will view us if we give up a sunk cost, anticipating that they will criticize us, blame us for not giving up sooner, or view us as a quitter.*[3]

From a Torah perspective, rational decision-making includes factors of the past as well. *Hakaras ha'tov* sometimes requires one to repay a favor even if it will not be beneficial to oneself in the future. If one has developed positive mitzvah habits, Hashem has high expectations that one will continue. We learned earlier in *Berachos* that if one usually davens in shul, and then one day he does not show up, Hashem inquires

---

1   *Sotah* 13b.
2   *Kesubos* 17a.
3   *Cognitive Therapy Techniques*, p. 190.

as to why he did not come.[4] If one has begun a mitzvah, that is an additional reason to see it to its completion. The Torah viewpoint is not identical to the viewpoint expressed by Leahy. There must be a balance of both commitment to our past decisions as well as logical decision-making going forward.

Try to see things to completion when it is logical to do so. Don't senselessly continue something just because you started it, but do include factors of the past, especially hakaras ha'tov, in your calculation.

---

4   *Berachos* 6a.

15a

RECIPE FOR OPTIMAL PRODUCTIVITY

רב חסדא לייט אמאן דמהדר אמיא בעידן צלותא.

Rav Chisda felt strongly [lit., "cursed"] that one should not search for water to do *netilas yadayim* when the time for davening has already arrived.

While the proper preparation for *tefillah* would include washing one's hands, Rav Chisda discourages us from searching for water once the time for *tefillah* has arrived.

There are times when it is preferable to begin by creating the ideal conditions for productivity, and there are times when it is preferable to just dive into immediate production.

When Yaakov travels to Mitzrayim to see Yosef, he sends Yehudah ahead to Goshen. *Rashi* suggests two interpretations:

- The first is that Yehudah was sent to create a place for Yaakov to settle and to instruct them, upon their arrival, how they should dwell. In other words, Yehudah was sent to set up a home for them where they could settle comfortably upon their arrival.
- The second interpretation is that Yehudah was sent to set up a *beis midrash* where they would be able to study Torah.

141

There is no doubt that Yaakov's ultimate goal was to facilitate the service of Hashem. The two interpretations differ only with regard to what the most effective approach would be. Should they begin by settling down comfortably so that they could devote themselves to Torah study under optimal conditions, or should they immediately begin the productivity of Torah study?

When the Jewish People reached Har Sinai on the first day of Sivan, Hashem did not give them any instructions because they were exhausted from their journey.[1] Hashem wanted them to first regain their strength and be in the optimal state of mind to receive the instructions necessary to prepare for receiving the Torah.

The Mishnah in *Avos* teaches us, "Do not say, 'When I have time I will learn,' because, perhaps, you will never 'have time.'"[2] The *Rambam* says, "Lest you say, 'After I have accumulated wealth or after I have acquired my needs, I will return to study.' If this thought enters your mind, you will never merit the crown of Torah."[3] We can't spend too much time setting up the ideal conditions, all the while neglecting our primary responsibility.

It is sometimes difficult to find the right balance between building ideal conditions and jumping straight into being productive. It is worthwhile to put thought into finding the correct balance.

Stephen Covey refers to this balance as the P/PC balance, which stands for Production/Production Capability. Covey writes:

> *This principle can be easily understood by remembering Aesop's fable of the goose and the golden egg. This fable is the story of a poor farmer who one day discovers in the nest of his pet goose a glittering golden egg...The farmer can't believe his good fortune. He becomes even more incredulous the following day when the experience is repeated. Day after day, he awakens to rush to the nest and find another egg. He becomes fabulously*

---

1   *Shabbos* 86b.
2   *Avos* 2:4.
3   *Rambam, Mishneh Torah, Talmud Torah* 3:7.

wealthy. But with his increasing wealth comes greed and impatience. Unable to wait day after day for the golden eggs, the farmer decides he will kill the goose and get them all at once. But when he opens the goose, he finds it empty. There are no golden eggs—and now there is no way to get any more. The farmer has destroyed the goose that produced them.

I suggest that within this fable is a natural law, a principle—the basic definition of effectiveness. Most people see effectiveness from the golden egg paradigm: the more you produce, the more you do, the more effective you are. But as the story shows, true effectiveness is a function of two things: what is produced (the golden eggs) and the producing asset or capacity to produce (the goose). If you adopt a pattern of life that focuses on golden eggs and neglects the goose, you will soon be without the asset that produces golden eggs. On the other hand, if you only take care of the goose with no aim toward the golden eggs, you soon won't have the wherewithal to feed yourself or the goose. Effectiveness lies in the balance—what I call the P/PC Balance. P stands for production of desired results, the golden eggs. PC stands for production capability, the ability or asset that produces the golden eggs.[4]

Both in spiritual and worldly matters, find the balance between jumping right into productivity and investing time to create the most conducive environment for optimal future productivity. Find the right P/PC balance.

---

4   *Seven Habits*, p. 61.

15a

THE POWER OF WORDS, THOUGHTS, AND UNDERSTANDING

רבי יהודה אומר משום רבי אלעזר בן עזריה: הקורא את שמע–צריך שישמיע לאזנו, שנאמר: שמע ישראל ה' אלקינו ה' אחד; אמר ליה רבי מאיר: הרי הוא אומר אשר אנכי מצוך היום על לבבך. אחר כונת הלב הן הן הדברים.

Rabbi Yehudah says in the name of Rabbi Elazar ben Azaryah, "One who is reading *Shema* must read it audibly, as it says, 'Hear, Yisrael...' Rabbi Meir replied, "The verse says, 'upon your heart' to teach that it is one's intent that is primary [and that *Shema* may be recited in one's heart without actually hearing the words].

Rabbi Meir says that ultimately, it is not whether or not the *berachah* is audible that is important. What matters most is that one has the proper intention. This is a very sensible position. Why do the other Tanna'im disagree?

The *Mishnah Berurah* writes that when one purchases food for Shabbos, one should say, "This is for the honor of Shabbos,"[1] because speech has a great effect on holiness.

Words have the power to infuse holiness, and words have the power to create mundane, yet important, realities as well. Stan Toler writes:

> *Your words have creative power. Let that sink in for a minute. The things you say take shape in your life and in the lives of those around you...Your words have the power to create or to destroy. Think about the effect your words may be having on you or your relationships right now in ways you haven't noticed. For example, when you're complaining, what's the effect on your attitude? On your workmates? On your children? What has been the effect of praise in your life? How have you responded when others complimented or affirmed you? How did it shape your attitude? Your thoughts? Your actions? How often do you exercise your word power? Do you tend to use that power positively, giving hope, encouragement, and affirmation to others? Or do you tend to use your power negatively, offering complaints, criticism, or insults? Your words have creative power; use them for good.*[2]

Surely, Rabbi Meir agrees with this concept as well. Surely, he also believes that words have tremendous power. If so, why does Rabbi Meir *pasken* that merely thinking the words with the proper intent is sufficient?

Rav Levi Yitzchak of Berditchev, at the beginning of *Pirkei Avos*, explains that every person has their own innate approach to serving Hashem. The basis of that approach, the "*av*" (lit., "father"), is the basis for their various *piskei halachah* in learning as well. *Pirkei Avos* is so-named because each Mishnah teaches us the foundation of each Tanna's approach to serving Hashem, which then expresses itself in all of their teachings throughout *Shas*. As an example, Rav Levi Yitzchak quotes

---

1   *Mishnah Berurah* 250:2.
2   *The Power of Your Attitude*, p. 32.

many rulings of Rabbi Meir where he emphasizes the significance of one's thoughts. Rabbi Meir's approach to serving Hashem, says Rav Levi Yitzchak, is from the "world of *machshavah* (thoughts)."

Knowing that everyone has their own foundational approach to doing good can help us judge others favorably. In explaining the premise of Cognitive Behavioral Therapy, Dr. Judith Beck states that a person's actions always make sense when we understand the thoughts and perspectives from which they arise.

Contemplate the power and effect of your words. Know that everyone comes with their own approach and perspective, and from within that standpoint their actions and views make sense.

16a

FOCUS ON THE MISSION: THE SETBACKS CAN BE OVERCOME

למה נסמכו אהלים לנחלים, דכתיב: כנחלים
נטיו כגנות עלי נהר כאהלים נטע וגו', לומר לך—
מה נחלים מעלין את האדם מטומאה לטהרה—
אף אהלים מעלין את האדם מכף חובה לכף זכות.

Why [does the the Torah] juxtapose "tents" (*Rashi*) to "streams"? To teach that just as a stream purifies a person [as a mikvah], so too tents of Torah raise a person from guilt and make him meritorious.

Learning Torah has the ability to purify and elevate a person from the status of being guilty to being meritorious. What this means for us is that if we feel that we have done something wrong, learning Torah is a way to clean our slate and transform ourselves.

How much Torah must we learn to have this profound effect? Chazal say that one who has sinned should increase his learning.[1] If

---

1   *Vayikra Rabbah* 25:1.

he is accustomed to learning one chapter, he should begin to learn two chapters. This small increase in learning is sufficient to make a person meritorious. There is no need to become overwhelmed if we have done something wrong. It is much more productive and pleasant to constructively add to our learning instead.

The Gemara in *Yoma* teaches that on Erev Yom Kippur, they would show the Kohen Gadol the various animals that he would be offering the following day to familiarize him with the service.[2] The Mishnah omits the goats that were brought as sin offerings. The Gemara explains that they would not show the Kohen Gadol the goats of the sin offerings because of a concern that he may become overwhelmed or depressed. The Gemara then questions why they showed him the bull that was also brought as a sin offering. The Gemara answers that since the bull was a sin offering only on behalf of the Kohanim, if any Kohen had sinned, the Kohen Gadol would be aware of it and would be able to assist him in doing *teshuvah*. Thus, the Kohen Gadol would not become overwhelmed or depressed. The goats, however, were sin offerings for the entire nation, and the Kohen Gadol would have no way of ensuring that all the sinners of the nation did *teshuvah*.

We learn from this discussion that as long as one knows what wrong was committed, and that one is prepared to improve, there is no reason to feel overwhelmed or depressed. One simply corrects the wrong and moves forward.

When Yosef is sent to inquire of his brothers' welfare, they plot to kill him. Reuven, intending to save Yosef and return him to his father Yaakov, suggests that they instead throw him into the pit. When Reuven returns and learns that Yosef has been sold into slavery, he is distraught. Where was Reuven when Yosef was sold? *Rashi* tells us that he had gone to fast and wear sackcloth to do *teshuvah* for having moved Yaakov's bed.[3]

Reuven was in the middle of an important mission to save his brother Yosef and return him to his father. He became sidetracked by a feeling

---

2   *Yoma* 18a.

3   *Bereishis* 37:29.

that he must repent now for a previous misdeed. He abandoned his watch, and as a result Yosef was sold into slavery.

We all are in the midst of an important mission of continuing to grow in Torah and mitzvos. That is why we exist. We'll have successes and failures. When we make a mistake, there is a mitzvah of *teshuvah*. It is fulfilled by acknowledging the error, regretting having committed it, and resolving not to repeat it.

Rav Hadar Margolin cites the following excerpt from Rav Shlomo Wolbe. "When the evil inclination attacks us, we are ashamed of ourselves...We thought of ourselves as people of stature—and this [our sin] arouses in us a degraded feeling that demolishes our sense of self-worth."[4] Rav Margolin explains, "In other words, our feeling of sadness may not come from our pain over the severity of the sin itself, but rather from the loss of our self-worth...Sadness and disappointment in ourselves...are not emotions rooted in fear of Hashem, but rather in personal pride...This sadness is not the emotion on which the mitzvah of *teshuvah* can be based."[5]

After having fulfilled the mitzvah of *teshuvah*, it is essential that we not become overwhelmed or depressed in a way that would distract us from our continuous mission to grow in Torah and mitzvos.

Learning Torah purifies us. Don't be overwhelmed. Repentance isn't difficult. Don't let negative feelings of guilt distract you from your continuous responsibility to grow.

---

4 *Alei Shur*, vol. 1, p. 35.
5 Rabbi Hadar Margolin, *Crown Him with Joy* (Targum Press, 2007), p. 29.

16a

VALUE TIME WITH JOY

רבי אמי ורבי אסי הוו קא קטרין ליה גננא לרבי
אלעזר, אמר להו: אדהכי והכי איזיל ואשמע מלתא
דבי מדרשא, ואיתי ואימא לכו...אתא ואמר להו.
אמרו ליה: אלו לא באנו אלא לשמוע דבר זה—דיינו.

Rabbi Ami and Rabbi Asi where tying a chuppah in preparation for Rabbi Elazar's wedding. Rabbi Elazar said to them, "In the meanwhile, I will go and hear Torah in the *beis midrash*, and then I will return and relate it to you."...He returned and repeated what he had learned. They said to him, "If we had only come to hear this, it would have been sufficient."

Rabbi Zelig Reuven Bengis completed *Shas* with such regularity that his family became accustomed to the regular and constant *siyums* that he would celebrate. His family was surprised, however, when several months after his previous *siyum haShas*, he announced that he would be celebrating another *siyum haShas* in the coming days. He explained to them that for years he has taken his small Gemara with him so that whenever he finds a few extra minutes he can learn. He began with *Masechta Berachos*, and was about to complete *Shas* in that *seder limud*.

In the biography of Rav Elyashiv, *Amudo Shel Olam*, Rav Yisraelson describes his grandfather's commitment to using every moment for studying Torah. He writes:

> *Every moment of his life was counted and measured. We could see tangibly how he counted his seconds so that no small amount of time would be wasted. Nonetheless, his face always shone with a pleasantness that created a nice atmosphere for everyone around him...Seemingly, this is impossible. When a person experiences a tension and a fear of wasting time, it usually makes those around him uncomfortable. Rav Elyashiv was different. He managed to successfully combine these two aspects in fulfillment of the verse, "Strength and joy is in His place."*[1]

How does one accomplish this feat? By valuing time with a positive perspective. If you think, "There is so much value and so much to be gained by using the time well," you will use the time joyously. If, however, you think, "It would be terrible to waste this time," you will feel an uncomfortable pressure to avoid this negative outcome of wasted time.

Let us joyously make the most of all of our blocks of time, no matter how small. And let us do it with the self-talk of how pleasurable it is to make such good use of time.

Value small blocks of time. Don't let this appreciation of time lead to stress and pressure. Instead, take joy in the knowledge that you have valuable time that you can now use for important purposes.

---

1   *Amudo shel Olam*, p. 265; translated from Hebrew.

16a

AVOID MIND-READING

רבי אמי ורבי אסי הוו קא קטרין ליה גננא לרבי
אלעזר, אמר להו: אדהכי והכי איזיל ואשמע מלתא
דבי מדרשא, ואיתי ואימא לכו...אתא ואמר להו.
אמרו ליה: אלו לא באנו אלא לשמוע דבר זה—דיינו.

Rabbi Ami and Rabbi Asi where tying a chuppah in preparation for Rabbi Elazar's wedding. Rabbi Elazar said
to them, "In the meanwhile, I will go and hear Torah in
the *beis midrash*, and then I will return and relate it to
you."...He returned and repeated what he had learned.
They said to him, "If we had only come to hear this, it
would have been sufficient."

Rabbi Ami and Rabbi Asi were doing Rabbi Elazar a favor by helping him prepare for his wedding. While they were busy working hard
to build his chuppah in preparation for the wedding, Rabbi Elazar told
them that he was leaving to go to the *beis midrash* to learn.

Was this decision to go to the *beis midrash* comfortable for Rabbi
Elazar? When the Torah commands us to help our friend unload his
donkey, the Torah says, "You must help with him." Chazal explain
that the Torah uses the words "with him" to teach that if he refuses

to participate, you are exempt from helping him.[1] Presumably, Rabbi Elazar needed help building the chuppah, and for whatever reason was unable to do so himself. Nonetheless, didn't he feel uncomfortable leaving them while they were doing him a favor? Did he perhaps think that keeping them company with small talk would have been more appropriate?

It's not always comfortable to do something that appears "very religious." It's not always comfortable to tell someone, "Now is the time for my learning. I am not able to discuss other matters now." We are sometimes afraid that others will be offended or will perceive us as arrogant. This is an example of the cognitive distortion of mind-reading. The Gemara in *Pesachim* teaches that a person does not know what his friend is thinking.[2] When Rabbi Elazar returned and related what he learned to Rabbi Ami and Rabbi Asi, they were thrilled that he had gone to the *beis midrash*. They exclaimed, "If we had only come to hear this Torah, it would have been sufficient." Many times, we are uncomfortable saying something to someone because we fear they will react negatively when in reality their reaction would be quite positive.

Rabbi Shimon Finkelman writes the following in the biography of the Manchester Rosh Yeshiva, Rav Yehudah Zev Segal:

> *As his renown spread, people viewed his diligence as something for which to strive. When, for example, he officiated at a marriage ceremony and studied from a Chumash at every spare moment, those assembled left with a heightened appreciation of the value of Torah study. However, in his early years as Rosh Yeshiva, there were those who saw his opening of a sefer at such instances as a manifestation of his excessive "frumkeit," his taking the requirements of halachah to an extreme. He once confided to a talmid: "Do you think it is easy for me? I know that there are those who see me with my sefer and think that I am too 'frum,' but I am not deterred by this. And why should I*

---

1   *Bava Metzia* 32a.
2   *Pesachim* 54b.

be?...I am obligated to use my available time for learning. As for any discomfort I might feel, I remind myself of the words of Rama in the opening passage of Shulchan Aruch [that one should not feel shamed by those who mock his service of Hashem]."[3]

We never know exactly what someone will think or how someone will react. As long as we are sure that we are doing what's right, we should go ahead with our decision.

Do what is right without being swayed by what you think people are thinking. In fact, we can never truly know what others are thinking. It is not worthwhile to engage in mind-reading.

---

3   P. 140.

16a

MINIMIZE ANXIETY BY EXPOSURE

תנו רבנן: האומנין...ומתפללין בראש הזית ובראש התאנה, ושאר כל האילנות–יורדים למטה ומתפללין. ובעל הבית–בין כך ובין כך יורד למטה ומתפלל, לפי שאין דעתו מיושבת עליו.

A worker may daven atop an olive or fig tree [because he is less afraid that he will fall because of their many branches]. If he is working on a different tree, he must descend in order to daven. The owner of the field must always descend because he will lack peace of mind [even while atop an olive or fig tree].

A worker in a field frequently climbs the trees to harvest its produce. He has become accustomed to this. He isn't afraid when standing at the top of a fig tree or olive tree. Its many branches provide ample room for him to stand and there are many supports for him to grasp. The owner of the field, however, does not have peace of mind while standing in a tree, even if it is a tree with many branches. He still is afraid that he may fall.

The Gemara in *Shabbos* teaches that we may not lay siege to an enemy city within three days of Shabbos.[1] The *Beis Yosef* quotes the *Rosh* and the *Rif*, who both explain that during the first three days of laying siege, the fear of war will interfere with one's ability to enjoy the Shabbos food. After three days, the fear becomes minimized and it is possible to enjoy the Shabbos meals.

What is the mechanism by which becoming accustomed to something decreases fear? Is it merely that we get used to it, or is it more than that?

Adrian Wells writes: "In anxiety treatment, behavioral experiments typically involve testing predictions concerning physical, social, or psychological danger. They require a combination of exposure to feared events plus disconfirmatory maneuvers that are intended to test out belief in thoughts."[2]

Fear is an emotion that is caused by thoughts and predictions of a negative outcome. A behavioral experiment involves putting yourself in that feared situation and having the opportunity to observe first-hand that the feared prediction does not come true. The fear dissipates only when you notice how the feared prediction did not materialize. For example, if you are afraid to fly on an airplane, just flying on the airplane multiple times will not in itself diminish the anxiety. You must become conscious of the thoughts and predictions of fear before the experiment. Following the experiment, you must be conscious of how the prediction did not materialize. After observing these facts multiple times, you cease to make the negative predictions that are contrary to the evidence and contrary to your experiences. You will then no longer fear the situation. This technique can be used to decrease anxiety in many areas of life.

Use exposure to overcome fear. Make sure to notice that your feared prediction did not come true.

---

1   *Shabbos* 19a.
2   Adrian Wells, *Cognitive Therapy of Anxiety Disorders*, p. 81.

16b

RESPECT AND HONOR OTHERS

וכשמת טבי עבדו קבל עליו תנחומין; אמרו לו
תלמידיו: למדתנו רבינו שאין מקבלין תנחומין
על העבדים! אמר להם: אין טבי עבדי כשאר כל
העבדים, כשר היה.

When Rabban Gamliel's servant Tavi passed away,
Rabban Gamliel accepted words of comfort. His students said to him, "Didn't you teach us that we do not
accept the formal words of comfort over the passing of
a servant?" He replied, "My servant Tavi is not like other
servants. He was a good and upstanding individual."

If a close friend passes away, none of the practices of mourning apply.
One only observes the laws of mourning when an immediate relative
passes away. Nonetheless, when an *"eved kasher,"* an upstanding servant, passes away, Rabban Gamliel teaches us that the master observes
one of the practices of mourning by receiving words of comfort. In some
respects, the servant is viewed as a member of the family.

The Mishnah in *Pirkei Avos* teaches us that man is precious because
he is created in the image of G-d, and that B'nei Yisrael are precious

because they are referred to as Hashem's children.[1] The *Tur* quotes the expression of Chazal, "The honor of Hashem's creations is a matter of great significance," and then adds that one certainly must treat the descendants of Avraham, Yitzchak, and Yaakov with great respect.[2] It is clear from the *Tur* that the expression of Chazal was not referring to only Jews but rather to all of humanity.

B'nei Yisrael are precious because they are referred to as Hashem's children.

The story is told that once someone told Rav Shlomo Zalman Auerbach that the Chazon Ish was waiting outside to speak with him. The Chazon Ish would rarely travel from B'nei Brak to Yerushalayim, and Rav Auerbach was eager to afford him the greatest respect. He set the table as he would for Shabbos and dressed in his Shabbos clothes to welcome in the *gadol ha'dor*. When he opened the door, he saw that it was not the Chazon Ish but someone who looked like the Chazon Ish. Rav Auerbach welcomed him in and treated him with the same respect that he would have shown the Chazon Ish. Those who had witnessed what had happened asked him why he had shown the man such great respect. He answered that, in truth, that is the respect due to every person.

This does not mean that every person deserves the same respect as the Chazon Ish. It was Korach who argued that everyone is of equal holiness, and that Moshe Rabbeinu should have no role of leadership over the Jewish People. Rather, what it means is that the range of respect that we show others, depending on who they are, frequently starts at a much lower point than it should. The respect that we show for the righteous may in truth be the degree of respect to which every human being is entitled, while the righteous themselves may deserve an exceedingly greater level of respect than we ever imagined.

The Mishnah in *Avos* states that the honor of one's student should be like his own honor, the honor of one's friend should be like the awe he

---

1   *Avos* 3:14.
2   *Tur, Choshen Mishpat* 2.

feels for his *rebbi*, and the awe one feels for his *rebbi* should be like the awe he feels toward Hashem.[3]

The respect that we feel for the greatest people of the generation is really the respect that is due to everyone. The respect that we feel for Hashem Himself is the respect that is due to the great rabbinic leaders of the generation. And the respect that we must inspire ourselves to feel toward Hashem Himself is infinitely greater.

When we see another person, i.e., anyone who we see on the street, whether Jew or gentile, even if they are not in a role of importance, they carry the image of G-d and deserve the utmost respect.

---

*Every person was created in the image of G-d
and deserves great respect.*

---

3   *Avos* 4:12.

16b

MINIMIZE CRITICISM

אמר להם: כמדומה אני שאתם נכוים בפושרים,
עכשיו אי אתם נכוים אפילו בחמי חמין.

[Rabbi Eliezer's maid passed away, and his students
came to offer him the formal words of comfort that one
offers to someone who has lost an immediate relative.
When Rabbi Eliezer saw them coming, he walked away
because the formal words of comfort are reserved
for the passing of an immediate family member. The
students followed him and he continued to distance himself. Finally, he said to them,] "I thought that you would
understand a small hint. Now I see that you do not even
understand an explicit hint."

Rabbi Eliezer went out of his way to avoid having to tell his students that they had forgotten what he had taught them. His students'
relationship with him was primarily through the Torah that he taught
them, and to have forgotten it was, in a way, to have let him down. They
had great respect for their *rebbi*, and to feel that they let him down could
sap their motivation for continuing to grow in Torah. Rabbi Eliezer was

sensitive to this. It was extremely important for him to see to it that his *talmidim* would not feel hurt.

Dale Carnegie quotes Charles Schwab as having explained his successes by his efforts to show thoughtfulness to his employees:

> *I consider my ability to arouse enthusiasm among my people the greatest asset I possess. And the way to develop the best that is in a person is by appreciation and encouragement. There is nothing else that so kills the ambitions of a person as criticisms from superiors. I never criticize anyone. I believe in giving a person incentive to work. So, I am anxious to praise and loathe to find fault. If I like anything, I am hearty in my approbation and lavish in my praise.*[1]

Encourage people with positive motivation. Don't criticize.

---

1   *Win Friends and Influence People*, p. 23.

17a

HUMILITY IS NECESSARY FOR GROWTH

וְנַפְשִׁי כֶּעָפָר לַכֹּל תִּהְיֶה.

[When Mar, the son of Ravina, finished the formal text of davening, he would add his own short individual prayer (the text of *Elokai Netzor*, which is now included as the final paragraph of the formal text of davening). He said:]
"...My soul should be like dust before everyone..."

The simple understanding of the *tefillah*, "My soul should be like dust before everyone," is that we ask Hashem to enable us to acquire the trait of humility. *Tosafos*, however, suggests a different interpretation. He says that we are asking Hashem to make us indestructible like the dust. Just as dust cannot be destroyed, so too, our descendants should never be subjected to destruction.

Is there any connection between the simple understanding of the *tefillah*—a request for humility—and *Tosafos*'s interpretation—a request that we be indestructible?

The Gemara in *Sanhedrin* states, "A person should always be in darkness and survive."[1] *Rashi* explains that the Gemara is advising us to remain low-key and avoid positions of authority in order to live a longer life. Humility is central to living successfully.

While this may be due partially to spiritual and metaphysical reasons, it is also very practical and logical.

The Gemara says that one should always be soft as a reed.[2] In *Avos D'Rabi Nosson*, we learn that a reed can survive any onslaught of the wind. Since the reed is soft, it merely bends in the wind and then returns to its original stature.[3] Because of this trait, the reed was chosen as the ideal quill with which to write *Sifrei Torah*.

One who is tough or rigid and lacks humility will frequently find themselves in the heat of an argument or a competition. It will detract from his ability to study Torah or to grow in *avodas Hashem*. On the other hand, one who is humble, soft, willing to bend, agreeable, and ready to forgo what they might be entitled to will be saved from all of the potential impediments to peace of mind. He will be able to devote his attention entirely to Torah learning and growth, and will merit a longer and more succesful life.

Humility and flexibility are requirements for success.

---

1   *Sanhedrin* 14a.
2   *Taanis* 20a.
3   *Avos D'Rabi Nosson*, chap. 41.

17a

HAVE POSITIVE SECONDARY THOUGHTS

רבי יוחנן כי הוה מסיים ספרא דאיוב אמר הכי: סוף
אדם למות, וסוף בהמה לשחיטה, והכל למיתה הם
עומדים. אשרי מי שגדל בתורה ועמלו בתורה ועושה
נחת רוח ליוצרו.

When Rabbi Yochanan concluded the study of *Sefer Iyov*,
he said, "Ultimately man passes away, and ultimately
an animal is slaughtered. Everyone eventually dies.
Fortunate and happy is the person who has grown in
Torah and toiled in Torah, and has brought happiness to
his Creator.

The original thought of "everyone ultimately dies" could lead to very
divergent secondary thoughts. For some, the following thought might
be "everything is futile," "life is depressing," or "I may as well do whatever I want." For Rabbi Yochanan, the following thought was, "Happy is
one who has grown in Torah and who has pleased Hashem."

Whenever a thought begins to make us sad, we can ask ourselves
whether it is the fact of the original thought that saddens us, or perhaps

a follow-up thought that brings the emotion of sadness. We can then question whether the follow-up thought is necessarily true. Perhaps there is an alternative way of viewing it. The thought of "everyone ultimately dies" describes a fact that is neither negative nor positive; while death appears to be only negative, the truth is that death can be viewed as a bridge from this world to the ultimate world of spiritual pleasure where Hashem rewards those who served Him. It is the follow-up thought that "everything is futile" that brings sadness. We can question this follow-up thought by asking if it is true. Just because everyone ultimately dies, does it necessarily follow that everything is futile? Of course not! On the contrary—everything that we do is even more valuable because we will ultimately return to Hashem to receive our reward for all of our accomplishments. That is what led Rabbi Yochanan to exclaim, "Happy is one who has grown in Torah and who has pleased Hashem."

Notice if your original neutral thoughts lead to negative secondary thoughts. Try to think of a way to reframe the neutral thought as positive, neutral, or less negative than your original evaluation.

17a

THE TRUTH OF DIFFERING PERSPECTIVES

מרגלא בפומייהו דרבנן דיבנה: אני בריה וחברי בריה,
אני מלאכתי בעיר והוא מלאכתו בשדה, אני משכים
למלאכתי והוא משכים למלאכתו, כשם שהוא אינו
מתגדר במלאכתי כך אני איני מתגדר במלאכתו,
ושמא תאמר: אני מרבה והוא ממעיט—שנינו: אחד
המרבה ואחד הממעיט ובלבד שיכוין לבו לשמים.

The Rabbis of Yavneh would frequently say: I [the Torah
scholar] am a living being, and my friend [the farmer]is a
living being. I work in the city and he works in the field.
I arise early in the morning for my work, and he arises
early in the morning for his work. Just as he doesn't
envision taking up my work, so too I don't envision taking
up his work. And lest you say that I do much and he does
little, we have learned, "Whether one does much or little,
[it is equivalent] so long as his intent is for the sake of
Heaven."

Rashi and the *Maharsha* take different directions in explaining this Gemara. In fact, the differing worldview and ideologies of different Jews can perhaps be traced back to this foundational difference of opinion.

Rashi understands the Gemara as teaching that those working in the field are making the wrong choice. It would be preferable for them to remain in the *beis midrash* and learn Torah. Even though they would not accomplish as much in learning as the Torah scholars, they would be rewarded equally based on the principle, "Whether one does much or does little, it is all equivalent, so long as his intentions are for the sake of Heaven."

The *Maharsha* understands the Gemara as referring to those who work in the field for most of the day and spend a short time each day learning Torah, to the extent of their ability. Lest one think that the Torah scholars who spend the entire day learning will receive greater reward, the Gemara teaches that so long as the farmer's small amount of learning is for the sake of Heaven, he will receive equal reward. He has pushed himself to the limits of his ability for the sake of Heaven, and he will be equally rewarded.

The Gemara in *Eruvin* teaches that there are two palm trees in the Valley of Ben Hinom. Smoke rises from between them, and it is there that the entrance to *Gehinom* is found.[1] The *Maharsha* explains that palm trees, which produce honey from the dates, are symbolic of the pleasures of this world. The Gemara intends to warn us that one who excessively pursues the pleasures of this world will find himself approaching the entrance to *Gehinom*. It is important to keep in mind that when the *Maharsha* speaks of one who receives equal reward for learning part of the day to the extent of his ability, he is not referring to one who has the ability to learn more and instead prioritizes chasing after the pleasures of this world. Every person must make an honest calculation with themselves as to what their ability truly is.

---

1   *Eruvin* 19a.

Rashi's approach encourages everyone to involve themselves in full-time learning, regardless of whether they believe that they are "cut out for it." The worst-case scenario is that they will be less successful in learning, but they will receive equal reward for their efforts. The *Maharsha*, on the other hand, encourages everyone to assess their own abilities in learning and to determine, based on that assessment, how much of their day should be devoted to learning.

A similar example of differing worldviews and ideologies that are both legitimately sourced in the same text can be found in a *Rashi* on the following Mishnah in *Pirkei Avos*. The Mishnah states, "Not all of those who engage in excessive business will become wise."[2] *Rashi* suggests two interpretations. The first is that such a person "will not become wise in Torah." The second interpretation is that "one who wishes to become wise must involve himself in all areas of furthering the development of the world, both in business and in other wisdoms of the world, so that he will understand everything."

There are certainly ideologies that are contrary to the Torah. The *Biur Halachah* writes that the admonition we recite in the *Shema*, "You shall not stray after your heart," refers to heresy, which includes any ideology that is contrary to Torah.[3] We must not get caught up in the version of non-judgmentalism that does not believe in an objective right and wrong. At the same time, it is important to recognize that there is truth in multiple perspectives.

One prominent modality of therapy is called Dialectical Behavioral Therapy (DBT). The foundational principle of this type of therapy is "dialectics." Dialectics means:

> *A method of examining and discussing opposing ideas in order to find a synthesis...that no one [other than Hashem and His Torah—E.A.] has the absolute truth in a situation, so we need to allow ourselves to see truth in both sides of an argument...We may find ourselves using the words "always" or*

---

2   *Avos* 2:5.

3   *Biur Halachah* 1:1.

"never" when we get into a discussion or argument. When we
do that, we wind up taking one extreme position, digging our
heels in, on the side that we believe is completely right—and
believing that other people are completely wrong. What usually
happens then is an argument that nobody wins. Everyone just
digs deeper into his or her position...There is always more than
one way to see a situation...Accept that different opinions can
be valid, even if you do not agree with them.[4]

The Gemara in *Gittin* relates that Rabbi Evyasar and Rabbi Yonasan had differing interpretations of a verse in *Navi*. Rabbi Evyasar saw Eliyahu the Prophet and inquired, "What is Hashem currently doing?" Eliyahu replied, "He is studying that passage in *Navi* [that you and Rabbi Yonasan differ in]...and saying, 'My son Evyasar explains like this, and My son Yonasan explains like that." Rabbi Evyasar asked, "Is it, G-d forbid, possible that Hashem Himself is unsure?" Eliyahu answered, "Both of your opinions are the word of the living G-d." Eliyahu then went on to explain why both of their explanations to the verse in *Navi* had aspects of truth to them.[5]

Multiple perspectives can be legitimate. Different segments
of our broader community differ with regard to certain important
aspects of their worldview. Both perspectives have legitimacy
based on classic Torah sources.

---

4   *DBT Skills in Schools*, p. 61.
5   *Gittin* 6b.

PEREK 3

17b

NOURISH THE SELF-ESTEEM
OF OTHERS

מי שמתו מוטל לפניו—אוכל בבית אחר.

If one's deceased relative is before him, he must eat in
another house.

Eating in front of the deceased is a violation of the *pasuk*, "One
who mocks a poor man insults his Creator."[1] It is tantamount to teasing
the deceased, who is no longer able to enjoy the pleasure of food. Not
only is teasing the deceased a violation, but even refraining from giving
him the honor that he would desire can be a violation. The Gemara
teaches on the next *amud* that one who sees a funeral procession and
does not join the escort is also "mocking a poor man." If this is true with
regard to the deceased, then it is certainly true with regard to the living.

If we think about our own personal feelings, we will recognize that we
sometimes feel slighted or hurt if we don't receive the honor that we
expected to receive, even if nothing was said or done to insult us.

The Gemara later (18b) relates that the great Tanna, Levi, was punished by being excluded from the heavenly yeshiva because he hurt

---

1   *Mishlei* 17:5.

Rabbi Efes's feelings by not attending his *shiur*. Everyone, even someone as great as Rabbi Efes, needed to know that his *shiur* was appreciated. To refrain from providing that honor and appreciation for someone who needs it is equivalent to "mocking a poor man."

Dale Carnegie writes, "We nourish the bodies of our children and friends and employees, but how seldom do we nourish their self-esteem? We provide them with roast beef and potatoes to build energy, but we neglect to give them kind words of appreciation that would sing in their memories for years like the music of the morning stars."[2]

Be sensitive to the feelings and self-esteem of others.
Try to provide them with the appreciation that they crave.

---

2   *Win Friends and Influence People*, p. 25.

18b

LEADERS EMPOWER OTHERS

רב פעלים מקבצאל—שריבה וקבץ פועלים לתורה.
[The *pasuk* discusses the attributes of Benayahu ben
Yehoyada, the leader of the Sanhedrin in the time of
Shlomo HaMelech. The *pasuk* says that he was a man]
"of great accomplishment, from the place of Kavtzi'el."
[Chazal derive from these words] that he "increased and
gathered workers on behalf of the Torah."

Stan Toler writes:

*Leaders expand their work by multiplication, not just by
addition. An experienced leader is always on the lookout for
a talented newcomer. Leaders know they are limited by time
and space to meet all the needs of the organization. Adding an
additional worker may not be enough, however. New teams
will have to be formed. New workers will have to be recruited.
One of the first lessons of leadership is that one person cannot
do everything. But everything that needs to be accomplished*

can be accomplished through the recruitment, training, and empowering of others.[1]

Benayahu ben Yehoyada "increased and gathered workers for the Torah." The *Yaavetz* explains that "workers for the Torah" refers to those who toil in the study of Torah."

Studying Torah benefits the individual who studies, but it is also necessary for the Jewish People as a whole. The Gemara in *Bava Basra* teaches that if the entire Jewish People study Torah, we will be instantly redeemed from *galus*. The *Bach*, in a beautiful piece on *Birkas HaTorah*, teaches us how the study of Torah causes the *Shechinah* to descend to our world and light up the entire world with a powerful, spiritual light. We collectively need every individual's Torah study to infuse the world with the greatest degree of holiness and closeness to Hashem. This is something that cannot be done alone. It is a mission that requires us to recruit others to participate and work toward the goal.

The Gemara in *Bava Metzia* relates a story about the greatness of Rabbi Chiya. Rabbi Chiya saw that the Torah was becoming forgotten. He went to great lengths to teach one of the five *Chumashim* to each of five children, and one of the six orders of the Mishnah to each of six children. He then instructed each child to teach the others what he had learned. Rabbi Chiya was ultimately successful in solidifying the Torah knowledge of his generation. The Gemara concludes this story by saying, "This is why Rebbi exclaimed, 'How great are the deeds of Rabbi Chiya!'"[2]

Recruit and empower others. We need everyone's collective effort.

---

1   Stan Toler, *Minute Motivators*, p. 109.

2   *Bava Metzia* 85b.

19a

IGNORE UNWARRANTED DISAPPROVAL

דידעי ולא איכפת להו.

The deceased are aware [when they are criticized after their passing], but it does not bother them.

Rav Elyashiv was once walking with one of his sons when his son noticed a sign posted to the wall that contained very harsh and disrespectful words about Rav Elyashiv. His son observed that his father noticed the sign and continued walking without any change in his facial expression or demeanor. Impressed by his father's humility, he asked his father, "Didn't you see what they wrote about you?" Rav Elyashiv replied, "Anything that's not written in the Talmud means nothing to me."[1]

The deceased may know what was said in this world, but it is meaningless to him. They are already aware of what is truly important, and from such a heavenly perspective, insults are meaningless. The righteous are able to attain this exalted level even in this world because of their keen perception of what is truly important.

---

1   *Amudo shel Olam.*

The Gemara in *Gittin* says, "Those who are insulted but do not insult others, who hear themselves being disgraced and do not respond in kind, who do mitzvos out of love and are content even amidst suffering, about them the verse says, 'And those who love him are as the sun emerging in its strength.'"[2] The Gemara links tolerance toward insults to serving Hashem out of love. One who loves Hashem understands what is truly important and is not disturbed by the lack of respect that they receive from others.

Perhaps there is another lesson that we can learn from this Gemara in *Gittin*.

Why is it that one who does not respond to insults merits being compared to the sun as it emerges in its strength? On a basic level, the comparison connotes strength and power, an apt description for someone who exhibits such self-control. Perhaps there is an additional deeper explanation based on the following Gemara in *Nedarim*. There it relates that when Korach and his followers rebelled against Moshe Rabbeinu's leadership, the sun and moon rose to the highest heavens. They said to Hashem, "Only if you carry out justice [against Korach] on behalf of Moshe will we continue to provide light [for the world]." Hashem replied, "Every day there are idolaters who worship you, and you never objected on behalf of the respect due to Me. Why now are you so insistent on behalf of the respect due to a mere human?"[3] The Gemara tells us that from that day forward, the sun and moon only emerge to provide light for the world after they are coerced by heavenly arrows. *Rashi* explains that henceforth they refused to provide light as a sign of protest toward the idolaters who worship them. In other words, they accepted Hashem's rebuke. They now stand up on behalf of Hashem's honor as well.

Let's contemplate this. The sun stood up for what it believed was right. It had to protest against the slight to Moshe Rabbeinu's honor. It then faced intense Heavenly rebuke for not doing what was right in additional circumstances as well. Many people in this situation would

---

2   *Gittin* 36b.

3   *Nedarim* 39b.

not be receptive to such rebuke. They would feel that they did something good and shouldn't be the subject of criticism just because they could have done more. But the sun, in its strength, accepted the rebuke and internalized it. Perhaps this is why someone who does not respond to criticism is compared to the sun emerging in its strength to provide light for the world. If the criticism is valid and has merit, while it may not be easy to accept, one who is truly strong and humble will find ways to incorporate the rebuke and grow from it. Such was the power of the sun, and such is the power of one who is truly so humble.

Richard Carlson writes:

> *One of the most unavoidable life lessons is having to deal with the disapproval of others...The truth is, everyone has their own set of ideas with which to evaluate life, and our ideas don't always match those of other people. For some reason, however, most of us struggle against this inevitable fact. We get angry, hurt, or otherwise frustrated when people reject our ideas, tell us no, or give us some form of disapproval. The sooner we accept the inevitable dilemma of not being able to win the approval of everyone we meet, the easier our lives will become. When you expect to be dished out your share of disapproval instead of struggling against this fact, you'll develop a helpful perspective to assist your life journey.*[4]

Know what is truly important and don't be overwhelmed by criticism. Nobody attains everyone's approval. If there is truth to the criticism, learn and grow from it. If not, it is meaningless and don't let it disturb you.

---

4   *Don't Sweat the Small Stuff*, p. 87.

19a

NOTICE NUANCES: DON'T LABEL

והמטים עקלקלותם יוליכם ה' את פועלי האון שלום
על ישראל.

[The Gemara teaches that one who speaks negatively about Torah scholars, even after their passing, will fall into *Gehinom*, as the *pasuk* says,] "But those who turn to their crookedness, Hashem will lead them with the sinners; peace upon Israel."

Rashi explains the derivation: The previous *pasuk* was discussing good people, and this *pasuk* then says that those who turn to focus on the sins of these good people will be brought to *Gehinom* together with the sinners.

While the merits of the righteous far outweigh their flaws, there is nobody who is perfect. Every person contains a mixture of positive and negative character traits, and every person has performed both good and bad deeds. The righteous find themselves toward the positive end of the spectrum, whereas the wicked find themselves toward the negative end. The rest of us are all somewhere in between.

In the *piyut* of *Odeh LaKeil*, which some recite on Shavuos morning, there are two adjacent stanzas that express this point. The *piyut* begins by discussing how precious the *neshamah* of a person truly is. "Pay atten-tion to the *neshamah*, it is like precious stones, its light is like the light of the sun, seven times the light of the morning." The *piyut* continues by describing that every night the *neshamah* rises to heaven to give an accounting of its day. The next stanza says, "He finds it filthy, from sin and more…" The following stanza says, "He finds it adorned with tallis and tefillin, like a bride who is adorned."

It is easy to label ourselves or other people with global descriptions. It is difficult to see all of the nuances, recognizing both virtues and faults and the degree to which each are present. But the truth is that everyone is a composite of a myriad of traits and actions. "Labels" rarely give a person a complete perspective. In fact, labeling oneself negatively is one of the most common forms of cognitive distortions.

The Mishnah in *Pirkei Avos* teaches, "Judge everyone favorably."[1] It can also be read, "Judge the entire person favorably." In order to judge someone, or ourselves favorably, we must see the entire person. Similarly, the verse states, "Then I will not be embarrassed, when I look at all of Your commandments."[2] There may be some mitzvos that we have not fulfilled as well as we would have liked. If we focus on only those misdeeds, we may become embarrassed. When we focus on all of the mitzvos in their entirety, we recognize that for the most part we are good people.

Nobody is perfect. Judge yourself favorably. Don't adopt negative labels or globalize your specific shortcomings.

---

1   *Avos* 1:6.
2   *Tehillim* 119:6.

19a

HASHEM'S LOVE
FOR EVERY PERSON

יהי רצון מלפניך ה' אלקינו שתגדור פרצותינו ופרצות
כל עמך בית ישראל ברחמים.

[The text of *tzidduk ha'din*, which is recited when a relative passes away, includes the *tefillah*:] "May it be Your
will, Hashem, to rebuild our breaches and the breaches
of Your nation, Israel, with mercy."

Rav Yitzchak Zilberstein, in his book *Mitzvos B'Simchah*, relates the
following story that he heard from Rav Shach.

*Rav Chaim Ozer Grodzhinski, one of the leading rabbis of the
generation, once developed an intense shoulder pain and was
forced to travel to another city for medical care. The journey
did not go as planned, and Rav Chaim Ozer was forced to spend
Rosh Hashanah in a small town that barely had a minyan of
Jews. On Erev Rosh Hashanah, he noticed a certain man in the
town who was dressed differently from the other townsfolk. It
appeared as if he was from America. Rav Chaim Ozer greeted
him and inquired about where he was from. Sure enough,*

he was from America. The man explained that recently his brother, who lived in the town, had passed away. He had come from America to perform the mitzvah of yibum by marrying his late brother's widow. As the conversation continued, the man mentioned that his late brother and widow had been blessed with a large family and many children. The man did not know that in such a case there is no mitzvah of yibum, and that, in fact, were he to marry the widow, he would be in violation of a very severe Torah prohibition. Rav Chaim Ozer attempted to explain this to the man, but the man refused to listen. Only when Rav Chaim Ozer informed the man that he was the rabbinic leader of world Jewry did the man finally agree to accept the halachah. When Rav Chaim Ozer later related the story to Rav Shach, Rav Shach replied, "Apparently, Hakadosh Baruch Hu is willing to give the greatest Torah leader of the generation an intense shoulder pain and relocate him from a major Jewish city to a small town for the holy day of Rosh Hashanah all so that a very simple Jew who didn't even know basic Torah law would refrain from violating a prohibition. Such is the love that Hashem has for every member of Klal Yisrael!"

The text of the *tzidduk ha'din* includes a *tefillah* that Hashem should rebuild the breach in the Jewish People caused by the loss of the deceased. Every member of the Jewish People has a mission in life, and the entire Jewish People needs every individual. It is unfortunate when this is only recognized after someone's passing. It is wonderful when we have this recognition, about both others and ourselves, throughout our lifetime.

Every person is essential. Hashem has immeasurable love for every one of us.

19b

MAKE A KIDDUSH HASHEM

המוצא כלאים בבגדו פושטן אפילו בשוק, מאי
טעמא—אין חכמה ואין תבונה ואין עצה לנגד ה'—כל
מקום שיש חלול השם אין חולקין כבוד לרב.

One who discovers that his shirt contains *shaatnez* must remove his shirt, even in the marketplace. Why is this? The *pasuk* says, "Wisdom, understanding, and counsel are insignificant against Hashem." Whenever demonstrating honor to a person, even a great person, will result in a *chillul Hashem*, we do not show them honor. [Even though removing one's shirt detracts from one's honor, since to continue wearing a shirt with *shaatnez* is a *chillul Hashem*, we do not accommodate the person's honor.]

What is a more severe *chillul Hashem*—walking around in public without a shirt or wearing a garment that contains a trace of *shaatnez*? When a Jew walks around in public without a shirt, he is sending the message that he lacks a degree of self-respect. People may surmise that Jews are unimportant or unprofessional. Nonetheless, the Gemara

184

teaches us that it is a greater *chillul Hashem* to wear a garment that contains a trace of *shaatnez*.

There is a common misconception that the definition of *kiddush Hashem* is to appear important in the eyes of the nations, and the definition of *chillul Hashem* is to appear unimportant. While this is a valuable goal, it is not the definition of *kiddush Hashem*. Those who subscribe to this belief sometimes mistakenly believe that the more the Jewish People resemble the other nations of the world, the greater the *kiddush Hashem*. This is a very unfortunate mistake. We are not looking to sanctify our own honor. We are looking to sanctify Hashem's honor. When we demonstrate that we are willing to put ourselves down in the eyes of others (e.g., by removing the garment that contains *shaatnez*) in order that Hashem be elevated, that is a *kiddush Hashem*.

There is another common misconception regarding the definition of *kiddush Hashem*. This misconception is the idea that it isn't necessary to interact with the nations of the world in order to make a *kiddush Hashem* in their eyes. They will look at us from afar and appreciate the greatness of Hashem even without interacting with us. While in rare instances this may be correct, the following two sources in Chazal teach us of the great *kiddush Hashem* that arises from positive interactions with the nations of the world. In Moshe Rabbeinu's *berachah* to Shevet Zevulun, he says: "Nations will gather at the mountain, there they will offer righteous offerings."[1] *Rashi* explains that merchants from among the other nations will come to Eretz Yisrael to do business with Zevulun. Upon reaching the land of Zevulun, they will say, "Let's go a little further, to Yerushalayim, to see who is the G-d of the Jewish People and what He is like." There, they will see all of the Jewish People serving one G-d and eating the same foods (as opposed to other nations where different groups serve different gods and eat different types of foods). They will be so impressed with the unity amongst the Jewish People that they will exclaim, "There is no nation as great as this nation!" They will be inspired to convert, and that is why it says, "There they offer

---

1   *Devarim* 33:19.

righteous offerings." The *kiddush Hashem* is created as a result of the interactions between the people of Zevulun and the other nations.

The *Midrash Rabbah* relates that Rabbi Shimon ben Shetach once bought a donkey from an Arab merchant and discovered jewels attached to the donkey's neck. He returned the donkey to the Arab, who then exclaimed, "*Baruch Hashem*, the G-d of Shimon ben Shetach!"[2] This *kiddush Hashem* was only possible because of the interaction between Rabbi Shimon ben Shetach and the Arab merchant. Without interaction, the Jewish world would not be visible and open for the gentile world to observe.

When we engage the world and demonstrate the greatness, authority, kindness, and honesty of Hashem and His Torah, we sanctify His name in the world.

---

2   *Midrash Rabbah, Devarim* 3.

19b

LESSONS FROM
THE LAWS OF PURITY

אמר רבי אלעזר בר צדוק: מדלגין היינו על גבי ארונות
של מתים לקראת מלכי ישראל.

Rabbi Elazar bar Tzadok says, "We used to jump over the
coffins to run to greet the Jewish kings..."

The Gemara questions how this was permissible. Rabbi Elazar was
a Kohen, and Kohanim are forbidden from becoming impure. Anything
that passes over a dead body becomes impure, and by jumping over the
coffins, Rabbi Elazar would seemingly be violating this prohibition. The
Gemara answers that the coffin contained empty space above the body.
Based on the laws of purity and impurity, the impurity was therefore
contained within the coffin. The lid of the coffin prevented impurity
from rising to those who would travel above it.

Chazal learn from a *derashah* that a "*golel*" is impure. *Rashi* understands
that this refers to the lid of the coffin. *Tosafos* questions this definition.
There is a principle that anything that can receive impurity cannot block
impurity from transferring through it and making someone on the
other side impure as well. Since the lid of the coffin, according to *Rashi*,
is impure, the impurity of the *meis* should travel straight up through

the lid and transfer impurity to a person who jumps over the coffin. If *Rashi* is correct that the "*golel*" is the lid of the coffin, how could Rabbi Elazar have jumped over the coffin without becoming impure?

Tosafos answers that, according to *Rashi*, only the top of the lid becomes impure. The bottom of the lid, which is directly over the *meis*, remains pure. For this reason, the bottom of the lid, which is pure, prevents the impurity from ascending through it. (See *Tosafos* for why it is not problematic that Rabbi Elazar, who was a Kohen, touched the outside of the coffin which is itself impure.) *Tosafos* supports this suggestion by quoting a Mishnah in *Ohalos*, which states that if a barrel is used for the lid of the coffin, any liquids inside the barrel remain pure.[1] Clearly, the entire lid is not impure. Only the outer layer contracts the impurity of the "lid of a coffin."

The *Meleches Shlomo* explains that the source of the halachah that the lid contracts impurity is a *pasuk* that states, "on the open field."[2] Therefore, only the top of the lid, which is clearly visible and uncovered—"on the open field"—becomes impure.

The *Bartenura*, however, is troubled by the question of why the liquids in the barrel remain pure. Even if the impurity emerges from the top of the barrel, surely the entire barrel should become impure as a result (as it is all one vessel). He explains that the Mishnah is referring to a barrel made from earthenware. An earthenware vessel only contracts impurity from the inside. If impurity touches the outside, the inside and its contents remain pure. Though the *Bartenura* does not relate this idea back to *Tosafos*'s discussion, surely it is necessary to say that the outside of the coffin lid in *Tosafos*'s case was also made of earthenware. If it was not, when the outside of the lid produces the impurity of the "coffin lid," the entire lid should become impure because it is all one vessel. The only reason that Rabbi Elazar could jump over the coffin without becoming impure is because of the principle that an earthenware vessel only contracts impurity from the inside. What is the reason for this halachah?

---

1   *Ohalos* 15:9.
2   *Bamidbar* 18:16.

Perhaps we can suggest that an earthenware vessel is only considered to be significant due to the purpose that it serves. It is not inherently beautiful or valuable. Its only value is that it performs the function of containing items inside. The outside is, to some degree, considered insignificant. It is the paradigm of the Mishnah in *Avos* that one should look not at the vessel but rather at what it contains.[3] It is the lesson that externals are not nearly as important as internals. In the world of impurity, this is a common message. The essence of impurity (*avi avos ha'tumah*) is a dead body. The holy soul has departed, and all that remains is the external shell of the body. That external component is the source of impurity. The message of both the impurity of a dead body and the method in which an earthenware vessel contracts impurity is that we must focus on what is truly important and avoid the distractions of the externals.

An additional answer to *Tosafos*'s question is found in the *Rambam*. The *Rambam* writes that the lid of a coffin only becomes impure on a Rabbinic level. The *derashah* from the verse, "on the open field," is merely an *asmachta*. According to this position of the *Rambam*, it is clear why the lid can prevent the transfer of impurity, on a Biblical level, to those who travel over it.

The *Minchas Chinuch* provides a third answer to *Tosafos*'s question. He writes that on a Biblical level, even something that can contract impurity prevents impurity from transferring through it.[4]

On a Rabbinic level, the lid becomes impure, and thus impurity continues from the lid to anything else above it. Anything in its tracks that can contract impurity propels the impurity further. On a Biblical level, this is not so. An object that can contract impurity will become impure, but it does not propel the impurity further. One problem is not a catalyst for another. One problem is not a snowball rolling down the mountain and building on itself, becoming a dangerous avalanche. It is merely one problem that can be assessed and addressed independently.

---

3   *Avos* 4:20.
4   *Minchas Chinuch* 263.

Robert Leahy writes: "Unproductive worry often has this chain-reaction quality. You generate a series of negative consequences, each dependent on the previous negative consequence. Unproductive worry treats chain reactions as if they are highly probable outcomes. The real question, however, is, 'How likely is this chain reaction?' In most cases, it's highly implausible."[5]

---

*Externals are superficial. Focus on the internals of significance.
Unproductive worry frequently involves assuming one problem will lead
to another until a catastrophe develops. Don't allow minor worries
to snowball in your mind into highly unlikely scenarios.*

---

5   *The Worry Cure*, p. 72.

20a

SPECIALIZE IN WHAT
YOU FIND MEANINGFUL

מאי שנא ראשונים דאתרחיש להו ניסא, ומאי שנא
אנן דלא מתרחיש לן ניסא? אי משום תנויי—בשני
דרב יהודה כולי תנויי בנזיקין הוה, ואנן קא מתנינן
שיתא סדרי! וכי הוה מטי רב יהודה בעוקצין האשה
שכובשת ירק בקדרה ואמרי לה זיתים שכבשן
בטרפיהן טהורים, אמר: הויות דרב ושמואל קא חזינא
הכא, ואנן קא מתנינן בעוקצין תליסר מתיבתא! ואילו
רב יהודה, כי הוה שליף חד מסאניה—אתי מטרא,
ואנן קא מצערינן נפשין ומצוח קא צוחינן—ולית
דמשגח בן!

[Rav Pappa questioned,] "Why is it that miracles were
performed for the earlier generations and not for
us? If it's because of learning, in the generation of
Rav Yehudah they only focused on studying the laws
of damages, whereas we study all six orders of the
Mishnah. When Rav Yehudah arrived at the Mishnah that
states, 'A woman who pickles a vegetable in a pot...' or
'Olives that one pickled together with their leaves...' he

191

exclaimed, 'These Mishnayos are as difficult as the complicated questions of Rav and Shmuel,' whereas we have thirteen yeshivas that are studying these complicated Mishnayos. So why is it that when Rav Yehudah took off one shoe [as a sign of repentance], it immediately brought the needed rain, whereas we fast and cry out to Hashem and He does not listen?

Rav Pappa mentioned two examples of his generation's superiority in learning over Rav Yehudah's generation:

- The first example is that Rav Pappa's generation studied all six orders of the Mishnah, whereas Rav Yehudah's generation only studied *Nezikin*.
- *Rashi* and *Tosafos* differ as to how to understand Rav Pappa's second example. *Rashi* explains that Rav Pappa's generation understood thirteen perspectives to each *masechta*, including *Uktzin*, and Rav Yehudah's generation struggled to understand just one perspective. *Tosafos* disagrees and suggests that the advantage of Rav Pappa's generation was that it had many additional yeshivos studying *Uktzin*, with many *talmidim*.

We see here three different aspects of success in learning: breadth of knowledge, the analytical skills of understanding multiple interpretations of the same Mishnah, and the ability of the generation's teachers to present the Torah in a clear and appealing manner to draw many *talmidim* to Torah.

From the fact that Rav Pappa mentions these aspects of Torah study, we see that if not for any one of them, we would understand why Hashem miraculously answered the *tefillos* of Rav Yehuda's generation. (They excelled in an essential area of Torah that we would have thought Rav Pappa's generation had not attained.)

While all areas of Torah are important for everyone, you may feel a specific affinity for a particular method or subject of learning. Whether you prefer learning with breadth, depth, or sharing the beauty of Torah with others, your style of learning is of immense value. Chazal say that a person can learn most efficiently if he learns what his heart desires.[1] The Gemara in *Bava Basra* relates that Rebbi once addressed "those who study Chumash, those who study Mishnah, and those who study Gemara."[2] The *Rashash* observes that clearly, already in the time of the Gemara, there were people who studied Gemara but did not study Chumash or Mishnah. He rejects the critical attitude that some have for Torah scholars who are not well versed in the Written Torah. While it is true that *Rashi* teaches us that a Torah scholar must be knowledgeable in all of *Tanach*,[3] it is also true that one should focus on the areas of Torah where he feels the greatest attachment.

John Maxwell writes:

> *No one can go to the highest level and remain a generalist. My Dad used to say, "Find the one thing you do well and don't do anything else." I've found that to do well at a few things, I have had to give up many things. As I worked on this chapter, I spent time reflecting on the kinds of things I've given up. Here are the main ones: I can't know everyone...I can't do everything...I can't go everywhere...I can't be well-rounded...Ninety-nine percent of everything in life I don't need to know about.*[4]

Rabbeinu Yonah on *Avos* quotes a midrash to explain why Hashem did not divulge the reward that one receives for each particular mitzvah. The midrash relates a parable about a king who asked his servants to plant an orchard. He didn't tell them how much reward they would receive for planting each particular tree. If he would have told them, they would only have planted the most valuable of trees, and the orchard would have been lacking other trees and other colors that would have added to its beauty. Hashem desired that we be perfect and complete

---

1   *Avodah Zarah* 19a.
2   *Bava Basra* 8a.
3   *Shemos* 31:18.
4   John Maxwell, *How Succesful People Think*, p. 20.

with the performance of all of the mitzvos, and so He therefore kept hidden the reward of each particular mitzvah.[5]

When we speak about directing our focus to a particular area of our choice, we can't limit ourselves from the vast array of mitzvos and areas of Torah study that beautify our *neshamos*. Nonetheless, within our broad approach to creating the beautiful orchard of our *neshamos*, there is also room for selecting to focus on a particular area of Torah study or *avodas Hashem*.

The Gemara in *Megillah* tells us the secret of longevity of several Amora'im.[6] Each one was exceptionally particular about the performance of certain practices and mitzvos. Of course, they were devoted to the fulfillment of all of the mitzvos, but in addition they focused on a specific area in which they were exceptional. It was in this merit that they lived to such an old age.

Rabbi Chananya ben Akashya taught: Hashem desired to bring merit to the Jewish People. He therefore gave them a vast Torah and many mitzvos.[7] We benefit from every mitzvah, and none of the applicable mitzvos may be ignored. Nonetheless, great people have found an area where they have chosen to excel. We can learn from their example and devote additional attention to an area of our personal interest.

---

*Involve yourself in the full breadth of Torah and mitzvos
and find a specific area of interest in which to excel.*

---

5   *Rabbeinu Yonah, Avos* 2:1.
6   *Megillah* 27b.
7   *Avos* 6:14.

20a

CHALLENGES ARE FOR EVERYONE: YOU CAN SUCCEED

הוויות דרב ושמואל קא חזינא הכא.

[When Rav Yehudah would study difficult Mishnayos, he would exclaim:] "These are as difficult as the complicated questions of Rav and Shmuel."

Who would have imagined that the great Amora, Rav Yehudah, would have had difficulty struggling to understand a Mishnah?

Sometimes we think that we are the only ones who struggle with a particular difficulty. It appears so easy for everyone else. We are not privy to the inside information of what is truly going through the mind of the person who seems to be effortlessly accomplishing a difficult feat. If we were to ask them about their accomplishment, though, they might tell us of the tremendous strength, effort, and commitment that went into it. The unfortunate result of thinking that it's easy for everyone else is that we tell ourselves that we don't have the strength or brains to accomplish what they did. If we were to recognize that the other person experienced the same difficulty that we face and devoted all of their strength to succeed, we would be more willing to invest the same effort ourselves to bring about the same success.

In the introduction to *Portraits of Greatness*, vol. 2, Rabbi Mattis Goldberg writes,

> *Rabbi Mordechai Gifter, zt"l, as a young American bachur, like some of the readers of this book, hung on his wall a few pictures of the Gedolei Yisrael of his era. One picture frame, however, was left empty. When asked for the reason, he replied, "This frame I am saving for myself." Rabbi Gifter believed in himself, and indeed he became a gadol. His Torah education did not begin in a yeshiva, yet he became one of the greatest rosh yeshivas of his generation.*

Rabbi Goldberg continues by quoting from a speech delivered by another *gadol b'Yisrael*, Rav Yitzchak Sheiner, Rosh Yeshivas Kaminetz. Rav Sheiner said,

> *I perhaps am more American than many of you...I was brought up in America in Pittsburgh during the 1920's...I went to public school, Rogers Elementary School on Black Street up on the hill. I finished eight years of elementary school, and then I went to high school, like everyone in America. I went to Peabody High School on the other side of Maple Leaf Avenue—public high school, and everything that going to a public high school entails...*

Rav Sheiner goes on to describe how he found his way to a yeshiva in New York and ultimately how his life changed. [1]

This type of life story is not unique to Rav Sheiner. Countless Torah leaders began their lives as normal children growing up, and ultimately, they achieved greatness by facing the same challenges that we face, making the right choices, and investing effort and devotion to serving Hshem and to doing what's right.

Great individuals faced challenges very similar to the challenges that we face. Through making the right choices, they grew to greatness. We have the ability to do the same.

---

1   Rabbi Mattis Goldberg, *Portraits of Greatness*, p. 11.

20a

RELATIONSHIPS: FEELINGS AND ACTIONS

קמאי הוו קא מסרי נפשייהו אקדושת השם, אנן לא
מסרינן נפשין אקדושת השם.

The earlier generations sacrificed themselves for the
sake of Hashem and we do not.

Rav Yehudah's generation excelled at sacrificing for the sake of
Hashem. A willingness to sacrifice of oneself for the sake of another
demonstrates the great degree of love that one feels toward them.
Despite the high level of learning that Rav Pappa's generation attained,
they were not on the same exalted level as the generation of Rav
Yehudah, which had attained this level of love of Hashem.

The sefer *Achas Shaalti* asks the following question: The *Chovos
Halevavos* states that the greatest level that a person can reach is the
love of Hashem. The purpose of everything else, and even the purpose
of all of the mitzvos, is to bring a person to love Hashem. How, then,
are we to understand that the greatest mitzvah is the study of Torah?
Loving Hashem is itself one of the 613 mitzvos. If the *Chovos Halevavos*
is correct that all mitzvos are for the purpose of loving Hashem, surely
the greatest mitzvah should be to love Hashem and not to study Torah!

He answers that there is a difference between the mitzvah of loving Hashem and the level of being someone who loves Hashem. Any time that a person thinks about how much Hashem has done for him and how great Hashem is, and then has an emotional feeling of love for Hashem, he has fulfilled the mitzvah of loving Hashem. It is one of the six mitzvos that can be constantly fulfilled at any time. But someone who fulfills this mitzvah once is not considered an *"ohev Hashem,"* someone who is on the level of loving Hashem. The *Chovos Halevavos* says that in order to attain this level, one has to be devoid of any love for this world and its pleasures. So long as part of a person's focus is on worldly matters, there is a distraction that prevents him from attaining the level of an *ohev Hashem.* Similarly, there is a difference between the fulfillment of the mitzvah of studying Torah and the level of being a Torah scholar. The mitzvah is fulfilled every time that a person studies Torah, whereas the level of "Torah scholar" is only attained after years of consistent Torah study.

With this background, the *Achas Shaalti* explains that the greatest possible level that one can attain is to be an *ohev Hashem.* That is an even greater accomplishment than to be a Torah scholar. The purpose of all *middos* and mitzvos is to lead to loving Hashem.[1] Nonetheless, the greatest mitzvah is studying Torah. Studying Torah is the greatest mitzvah that one can do at any given time because it is the study of Torah that has the most powerful effect in bringing a person to love Hashem. It is even more effective than the fulfillment of the mitzvah of thinking thoughts of love for Hashem.[2]

Both in our relationship with Hashem and in our relationship with people, there are things that we do for the other and feelings that we have and can express toward the other. While our day-to-day schedule may revolve primarily around the things that we do, ultimately the more important aspect is the feelings that we have.

Expressing our feelings of love for Hashem and for people is more important than the specific things that we do for them.

---

1   See *Tomer Devorah* and Rav Matisyahu Soloman's introduction in *Matnas Chaim.*
2   Rabbi Yitzchak Joseph, *Achas Shaalti*, p. 109.

20a

BE PATIENT
AND JUDGE FAVORABLY

מתון מתון ארבע מאה זוזי שׁויא.

[Rav Adda bar Ahavah saw a Gentile woman wearing a garment that didn't meet the high standards of modesty that is required of Jewish women. Thinking that she was Jewish, he tore the garment from her. Since she was a Gentile, he was obligated to repay her for the garment and her shame. When she told him that her name was Massun, he exclaimed,] "Massun, Massun, cost me four hundred *zuz.*" [*Rashi* explains that the name "Massun" is related to the Hebrew word "*l'hamtin*," meaning to wait. Rav Adda was saying that if he would have waited and been more patient, it would have saved him four hundred *zuz.*]

The Torah tells us that Hashem descended to this world to see the tower of Bavel.[1] *Rashi* comments that Hashem is Omnipotent, and that it

---

1   *Bereishis* 11:5.

199

was not necessary for Hashem to "descend" to this world in order to see. Rather, Hashem's intent was to teach judges that they should not pass judgment until they see and understand exactly what the situation is.

The very first teaching of *Pirkei Avos* is "Be patient in judgment." Rabbeinu Yonah says that a person must remind himself that "those who rush will not have sufficient understanding, for mistakes are common amongst all people…when a person thinks about something a second time, he sees what he did not notice at first glance."

The process of judging others favorably involves two steps:

- The first is considering the possibility that they have, in fact, done nothing wrong.
- The second is considering that even if they have done wrong, perhaps there are behind-the-scenes factors that made it considerably more difficult for the person to do what is right.

Giving considerable thought to both of these possibilities requires patience.

The Hebrew word for patience is "*savlanus.*" Rav Shlomo Wolbe notes that the root of this word means to carry a burden. When someone mistreats us, or does something that we perceive as wrong or irritating, they become a disturbance; in a sense, a burden on our shoulders. We are tempted to throw off the burden in order to lighten our load. Patience, explains Rav Wolbe, is the willingness to invest that extra effort to carry that burden and not to throw it off.

Rav Wolbe's insight is helpful in applying patience to real-life situations. We all value patience, but sometimes the burden of being patient is too heavy. It is very difficult. We think to ourselves that "yes, patience is important, but not when it is a burden like this." Rav Wolbe is teaching us that it is precisely for situations where it is burdensome that patience is referred to as "*savlanus.*" These are the situations where we can actually demonstrate patience in the truest sense.

Have patience and judge favorably.

20a

RECOGNIZE AND APPRECIATE YOUR SKILLS

רבי יוחנן הוה רגיל דהוה קא אזיל ויתיב אשערי
דטבילה, אמר: כי סלקן בנות ישראל ואתיין מטבילה
מסתכלן בי, ונהוי להו זרעא דשפירי כוותי.

Rabbi Yochanan would sit at the gates of the *mikvah*. He
said, "When the Jewish wives return from the *mikvah*,
they will look at me and have children who are as good-
looking as I am." [Elsewhere in the Gemara, as well as in
the story of Yaakov Avinu caring for Lavan's sheep, we
see the idea that what a person sees before conceiving
children will affect the appearance of the children.]

Rabbi Yochanan recognized that he had a positive attribute that
he could use for a good purpose. With that recognition, he was able to
do a favor for many people. There are two important lessons here. One
is the importance of recognizing our skills, abilities, and positive traits,
and the second is the importance of using creativity to determine how
we can use these traits to benefit the community.

One of the animals whose hides was used in the construction of the *Mishkan* was the *tachash*. *Onkelos* translates *tachash* as the "*sasgona*." The Gemara in *Shabbos* explains that *sasgona* is an acronym for the Hebrew words that mean "it rejoices in its many colors."[1] If the very name and defining character of this animal was one of arrogance, would it have been the choice for the construction of the *Mishkan*, the very place where Hashem would come to rest His Presence? The Gemara in *Sotah* teaches that Hashem selected to rest His Presence on Har Sinai for the giving of the Torah, rather than on any of the other mountains, because of Har Sinai's humility.[2] Surely an animal with arrogance would not be chosen for the construction of the *Mishkan*. We must conclude that the *tachash*'s appreciation of its beautiful hides does not in any way contradict its humility. Its awareness that its beautiful hides could be used for the service of Hashem, in the building of the *Mishkan*, was laudatory. Perhaps this awareness is even the reason why it rejoiced in its many colors.

The Mishnah in *Avos* quotes Rebbi's exclamation that the proper path that a person should choose is one that brings glory to the one who follows it "and brings glory to him from people."[3] Rabbeinu Yonah comments, "One should beautify himself over the mitzvos with a beautiful lulav, tallis, and *Sefer Torah* in a way that people will glorify and praise him for them." The pride that this praise will engender is not considered to be a deficiency. Recognizing the honor that one possesses from following the path of Torah in a beautiful way is an essential component to serving Hashem with joy.

Dale Carnegie writes:

> *If you tell me how you get your feeling of importance, I'll tell you what you are. That determines your character. That is the most significant thing about you. For example, John D. Rockefeller got his feeling of importance by giving money to erect a modern*

---

1   *Shabbos* 28a.
2   *Sotah* 5a.
3   *Avos* 2:1.

hospital in Peking, China, to care for millions of poor people whom he had never seen and never would see. Dillinger, on the other hand, got his feeling of importance by being a bandit.[4]

---

*Recognize your skills, abilities, and positive traits,
and use them for good purposes.*

---

4   *Win Friends and Influence People*, p. 19.

20a

SELF-ESTEEM

עין שלא רצתה לזון ממה שאינו שלו—אין עין הרע
שולטת בו.

[The Gemara tells us that the descendants of Yosef
Hatzaddik are not affected by the evil eye. One of the
reasons given is that] "The eye that didn't want to
partake of what wasn't his [i.e., Yosef, who refused the
advances of Potiphar's wife], can't be dominated by the
evil eye."

The "evil eye" doesn't affect a person who did not want to take that
which did not belong to him. What is the "evil eye," and why does it not
affect such a person?

Rav Eliyahu Dessler explains that when a person flaunts his blessings
in a way that could make others jealous, Hashem reassesses whether
he truly deserves those blessings.[1] This is what Chazal mean by the
"evil eye."

Why would a person flaunt what they have, knowing that it will
make others feel the discomfort of jealousy? Usually, it is because

---

1   *Michtav Me'Eliyahu*, vol. 3, p. 314.

such a person needs others to recognize his superiority to compensate for a lack of true self-esteem. If he appreciated who he was as a person, his desire for the honor of others would not reach the point of making others jealous for the sake of achieving it. (It is a normal, positive emotion to want the respect of others. On *Shabbos Mevarchim*, we daven for a life of honor and wealth. If these were negatives, they would not have found their way into our *tefillos*. It is only when this desire becomes extreme and guides our actions in a negative way that it is problematic.) Ultimately, then, it is a person's lack of appreciation for his own blessings that leads Hashem to re-evaluate whether or not he truly deserves them.

While the mechanism of the "evil eye" is generated by flaunting one's blessings, there is another common malady that is caused by dissatisfaction that also leads to losing one's blessings. The Gemara in *Sotah* says, "Anyone who sets his eyes on what is not his is denied what he seeks, and what he does have is taken from him. This is what happened to the original snake…Kayin, Korach, Bilaam, Doeg, Achitophel, Gechazi, Avshalom, Adoniyahu, Uziyahu, and Haman. All of them wanted to take what wasn't intended for them and as a result, not only were they not given what they sought, they also lost what they had."[2] To continue to benefit from the *berachos* that Hashem has given us, we need to appreciate them.

Not only must we appreciate the *berachah* in order to avoid losing it, but Hashem does not even grant the *berachah* in the first place until a person appreciates it. *Rashi* in *Bereishis* tells us that Hashem did not bring rain until man came onto the scene and appreciated its value.[3]

With this understanding of the evil eye and of the connection between appreciation and mainting our blessings, we can understand why the evil eye doesn't affect Yosef's descendents. The evil eye harms only those who are not satisfied with what they have. Yosef, who did not want to take what was not his, is not affected by the evil eye.

---

2   *Sotah* 9a.
3   *Bereishis* 2:5.

How common is this lack of appreciation?

The Gemara in *Bava Metzia* tells us that Rav went to a cemetery and was able to discern that ninety-nine percent of those buried there died prematurely because of the evil eye.[4] A lack of satisfaction with who we are and the *berachos* that Hashem gives us is a widespread malady. If we did have this appreciation, we would be constantly happy. It is not an easy goal to accomplish, but it is well worth the effort.

How does one practically work on appreciating who he is as a person? What can a person do to build self-esteem?

Dr. David Burns writes:

> *The first step is to take a close look at what you say about yourself when you insist you are no good. [Dr. Burns is discussing an extreme case of lack of self-esteem, but the same can be applied whenever we unrealistically put ourselves down.] The evidence you present in defense of your worthlessness will usually, if not always, make no sense...You have been practicing for years and years the bad mental habits that helped create your low self-esteem. It will take systematic and ongoing effort to turn the problem around...Talk back to that internal critic...Train yourself to recognize and write down the self-critical thoughts as they go through your mind. Learn why these thoughts are distorted, and practice talking back to them so as to develop a more realistic self-evaluation system...This simple exercise of answering your negative thoughts with rational responses on a daily basis is at the heart of the cognitive method. It is one of the most important approaches to changing your thinking. It is crucial to write down your automatic thoughts and rational responses. Do not try to do the exercise in you head...You don't have to do anything especially worthy to create or deserve self-esteem;*

---

4   *Bava Metzia* 107b.

all you have to do is turn off that critical, haranguing, inner voice. Why? Because that critical inner voice is wrong![5]

Build your self-esteem by challenging your negative self-talk. With healthy self-esteem, you will appreciate the gifts that Hashem has given you and you will not feel a need to flaunt them.

---

5 *Feeling Good*, p. 57.

20b

GRATITUDE FOR EACH GIFT

וחייבין בתפלה דרחמי נינהו.

[Women are] obligated to daven [daily] because davening
is a request for Hashem's compassion [which women
need as well].

In our text of the Gemara, the Gemara suggests that one might have
mistakenly thought that women are exempt from *tefillah* because it is
a time-bound, positive commandment. *Rashi* does not accept this text
because the obligation to daven is Rabbinic, and this is not a "positive
commandment" of the Torah. *Tosafos* defends our text by arguing that
even a Rabbinically required, time-bound mitzvah is not obligatory for
women. *Tosafos* cites a Gemara in *Sukkah* that implies that women are
exempt from the mitzvah of reciting *Hallel*, presumably because it is a
time-bound, Rabbinic obligation.

Perhaps *Rashi* would defend his position by rejecting *Tosafos*'s proof
from *Hallel*. Perhaps *Rashi* would argue that *Hallel* is in fact a Biblical,
time-bound, positive commandment, and that is why women are exempt. The Gemara in *Megillah* says that, in theory, one should recite
Hallel on Purim. If we recite *Hallel* on Pesach, when we were brought
from slavery to freedom, then certainly we should recite *Hallel* on Purim
when Hashem saved us from death and granted us life! (In practice, we

do not say *Hallel* on Purim because, among other reasons, the reading of the *Megillah* is, in a sense, a form of *Hallel*.) The *Chasam Sofer* learns from here that there is a Torah obligation to praise Hashem in celebration of a miracle.[1] While the fact that Chazal selected *Hallel* as the text of this praise is merely Rabbinic, the recitation of *Hallel* is a fulfillment of the Torah obligation to commemorate the miracle with praise. If so, *Rashi* would argue that women are exempt from *Hallel* because it is a time-bound, Torah obligation.

This concept—that gratitude for Hashem's kindnesses and miracles must lead to additional praise and service of Hashem—is a theme in the classical mussar text, the *Chovos Halevavos*. There, it is written that one's duty to serve Hashem is commensurate with the favors that He has performed for him. This obligation, the *Chovos Halevavos* teaches, is dictated by logic and does not even require a *pasuk* from which to derive it. All of humanity has benefited from Hashem's kindness, and therefore everyone is obligated in the seven Noachide mitzvos that are clearly logical and are moral obligations. The Jewish People have received even more kindness from Hashem than the other nations of the world; Hashem took us out of Egypt and gave us the Torah and Eretz Yisrael. As such, we are required to observe a greater number of mitzvos to reciprocate to Hashem. The Kohanim and Levi'im, as well as the royal descendants of David HaMelech, have received additional gifts and are bound to observe even more mitzvos. The *Chovos Halevavos* adds that any individual who sees that Hashem is showering him with *berachah* is obligated to add to his service of Hashem out of a sense of gratitude.[2]

Gratitude and thanking Hashem for each wonder He performs for us are Biblical and even innately logical requirements.

---

1   *Chasam Sofer, Yoreh Deah* 233.
2   *Chovos Halevavos, Shaar Avodas Elokim* 6.

20b

A SENSE OF RESPONSIBILITY

וכל שאינו מחוייב בדבר—אינו מוציא את הרבים ידי
חובתן.

Someone who is not obligated in a particular mitzvah
can't fulfill the mitzvah on behalf of another person. [In
general, if someone is obligated in a particular mitzvah
that requires saying a blessing, such as reciting Kiddush
on Friday night, he can ask someone else to recite the
blessing on his behalf. Through listening to the blessing
recited by the other person, he has fulfilled his obligation. The Gemara here is teaching us that only someone
who is himself obligated in the mitzvah can fulfill it on
behalf of another person.]

One's ability to help someone else discharge their obligation is
based on the principle of "*arvus*."[1] Anyone who is obligated in a particular mitzvah has the additional responsibility to see to it that others also
fulfill their obligation. Someone who is not obligated in a mitzvah does

---

1   See the *Rosh* here in *Berachos*, and the *Tosafos Yom Tov* on *Rosh Hashanah* 3:7.

not have the responsibility to ensure that others fulfill their obligation and thus is unable to recite the *berachah* on their behalf.

While at first glance this appears logical, it is in fact difficult to understand. It's true that one who isn't obligated in a mitzvah doesn't have the responsibility to see to it that others fulfill the mitzvah, but why should that mean that he is unable to fulfill the mitzvah on their behalf?

The Gemara in *Avodah Zarah* states, "One who fulfills a mitzvah in which he is commanded and obligated is greater than one who fulfills a mitzvah that is optional."[2] *Tosafos* explains that one who is obligated "is constantly concerned to negate his evil inclination and fulfill the mitzvah of his Creator." There are two possible ways to understand *Tosafos*'s explanation. One possibility is that one who is commanded will have a sense of responsibility that will lead him to do a better job in fulfilling the mitzvah. The other possibility is that having a sense of responsibility can add pressure and make the fulfillment of the mitzvah more difficult. When a mitzvah is more difficult, there is greater reward for its fulfillment, as the Mishnah in *Pirkei Avos* teaches, "The reward is commensurate with the difficulty."[3]

Perhaps these explanations can shed light on why only someone who is obligated in a mitzvah can help another person fulfill their obligation.

The Gemara in *Bava Metzia* discusses a case of where Reuven asked Shimon to watch an object. Shimon, without Reuven's permission, then asked Levi to watch the object for him. Rav rules that Shimon is exempt from any damage to the object that incurred in a way that he would have been exempt had the damage happened while still under his watch (and Rabbi Yochanan disagrees). Abaye explains that this is certainly true if Shimon was an unpaid watchman and Levi was a paid watchman. Since a paid watchman has a greater degree of responsibility, Shimon was in fact *upgrading* the object's security by giving it to Levi. Abaye adds that Rav would exempt Shimon even in a case where Shimon was a paid watchman and Levi was an unpaid watchman. Despite the fact that Levi's responsibility is less and the security of the object has been

---

2   *Avodah Zarah* 3a.

3   *Avos* 5:23.

downgraded, it is still considered to be a sufficient level of protection to give over the object to another capable watchman.[4] We see from this case that an object's security is downgraded when it is given to someone with a lesser sense of responsibility. While Rav believes that this is not a problem when it comes to the obligation of a watchman, it may be a problem when it comes to selecting a representative to enable oneself to fulfill a mitzvah obligation. Because someone who is obligated in a mitzvah has a greater sense of responsibility, and therefore does a better job at performing the mitzvah, it is unacceptable to downgrade the performance of the mitzvah by passing it along to someone else with a lesser sense of responsibility.

Within the second explanation of *Tosafos* (that the added pressure of obligation adds to the difficulty and reward for the mitzvah's fulfillment), we can also understand why only someone who is obligated in a mitzvah can help another fulfill his obligation. Why is it that the reward for a mitzvah is greater when there is more difficulty to fulfill it? The most basic explanation is that Hashem's fair justice demands greater reward for more difficult service. Perhaps we can also suggest that a mitzvah fulfilled with greater difficulty demonstrates a greater love for Hashem. The *Midrash Tanchuma* on *Parashas Noach*, which speaks of the greatness of the Oral Torah, speaks of the difficulty involved in its study. It states that only someone who truly loves Hashem with all of his strength will commit to studying the Oral Torah. It is this greater expression of serving Hashem with love that earns the person the greater reward. If this is so, we can understand why only someone who is obligated in a mitzvah—and therefore has a greater level of difficulty to perform the mitzvah (due to the pressure and concern that he feels as a result of the obligation)—can exempt someone else from fulfilling their obligation. A mitzvah that is to be fulfilled by the individual who can demonstrate a greater love for Hashem cannot be passed on to someone who will fulfill the mitzvah in a way that demonstrates less love for Hashem.

---

4   *Bava Metzia* 36a.

The same is true in our relationships with other people. When we have a feeling of responsibility, we are more effective in helping others, and we convey more love and dependability.

It is important to have a sense of responsibility. You will do a better job and you will convey greater interest and care.

21a

THE SONG OF TORAH

מנין לברכת התורה לפניה מן התורה—שנאמר: כי
שם ה' אקרא הבו גדל לאלקינו.

What is the source for reciting a *berachah* before learning Torah? It is from the *pasuk*, "When I call the name of
Hashem, give greatness to our G-d."

The source for *Birkas HaTorah* is the *pasuk* from which we learn that
Moshe Rabbeinu said a *berachah* before beginning the song of *Haazinu*.

The Gemara in *Nedarim* teaches that the Jewish People were sent into
galus and Eretz Yisrael was destroyed because they did not recite *Birkas
HaTorah* before learning.[1] The *Ran* explains that not reciting *Birkas
HaTorah* was representative of the fact that the people didn't consider
Torah to be significant enough to warrant a *berachah*. The punishment
was not for the technicality of having omitted the *berachah*, but rather
for the perspective that devalued Torah to the point where no *berachah*
was recited.

If *Birkas HaTorah* demonstrates the value that we ascribe to the Torah,
then it is quite appropriate that the source for *Birkas HaTorah* is Moshe

---

1   *Nedarim* 81a.

214

Rabbeinu's *berachah* directly preceding the song of *Haazinu*. Song is an expression of great joy. It is something that is inherently valued.

The *pasuk* in *Parashas Vayelech* says, "And now, write this song for yourselves, and teach it to the People of Israel..."[2] The song mentioned here refers to the entire Torah. In fact, it is from this *pasuk* that we learn of the mitzvah to write a *Sefer Torah*. When we have the recognition that the Torah is a song to be sung with ecstatic joy and feelings of gratitude to Hashem, we will subscribe the greatest value to the Torah. Then we will say *Birkas HaTorah* with genuine enthusiasm and *simchah*!

Torah is like a song in the sense that we involve ourselves in it with joy.

---

2   *Devarim* 31:19.

21b

PARTICIPATE

ודכולי עלמא מיהת מפסק לא פסיק.

[Someone who is in the middle of *Shemoneh Esreh*] does not interrupt [in order] to answer *Kedushah* with the congregation.

Tosafos quotes *Rashi* in Sukkah that says that if a person is davening *Shemoneh Esreh* when the chazzan gets up to *Kaddish* or *Kedushah*, he should remain silent and listen. It is then considered as if he answered to the *Kaddish* or *Kedushah* based on the principle that "one who listens is as if he replied." Nonetheless, *Tosafos* says that this is not ideal. It is a greater "*hiddur mitzvah*" to verbally respond rather than to merely be considered as if one responded.

We are accustomed to thinking that *hiddur mitzvah* only relates to using a beautiful object for a mitzvah. We see from this *Tosafos* that *hiddur mitzvah* also applies to the degree in which a person participates in the mitzvah.

In *Atarah LaMelech*, Rav Pam elaborates on this point. He quotes the *Rambam* who says, "The joy that one experiences when performing a mitzvah, and the love for Hashem who commanded the mitzvah, is a great form of service of Hashem."[1] He then adds that this is, in fact, the greatest type of *hiddur mitzvah*!

There are two lessons that we can derive from this idea. First, we can enhance our joy and love for Hashem knowing that these thoughts and emotions add considerable value to the performance of the mitzvah. People go out of their way to seek out the most beautiful lulav and esrog, *Sefer Torah*, tallis, candlesticks, and other objects used in the performance of mitzvos. Certainly, all the more so, we should go to great lengths to appreciate the value of mitzvos so that we can perform them with great joy—the greatest *hiddur mitzvah*!

The second lesson is that participating is greater than merely observing. In Dialectical Behavioral Therapy (DBT), mindfulness is comprised of several skills, including observing, describing, and participating. Observing is being aware of both one's external surroundings as well as one's internal thoughts and emotions.

> *Describing is labeling what we have observed. Participating is entering wholly into an activity—spontaneously becoming one with the activity. It is throwing yourself into something. Participating wisely in the present moment without judgement is the goal of mindfulness....Participating is being fully present to our own lives, without self-consciousness, effortlessly in flow—forgetting ourselves and becoming what we are doing. Watch young children play. Whether they are running through a park, splashing in puddles, or dancing to music, children are great examples of participating. Participating is not thinking about yesterday or tomorrow. It is not worrying about what other people are thinking or feeling about us right now. It is about jumping into the current activity 100%.*[2]

Enjoying mitzvos is the greatest way to beautify them. Participate.

---

1   *Rambam, Mishneh Torah*, Lulav 8:15.
2   *DBT Skills in Schools*, p. 87.

21b

DO WHAT YOU CAN:
DON'T BE OVERWHELMED

זב שראה קרי, ונדה שפלטה שכבת זרע, המשמשת
וראתה דם צריכין טבילה.

[Different forms of impurity require different dura-
tions of time before the person may go to the mikvah to
regain purity. Someone who has contracted an impurity
that remains for seven days, and then contracts another
impurity that will remain for only one day, must go to the
mikvah to purify himself from the minor impurity. This
is despite the fact that the major impurity remains and
the individual is still considered to be impure.]

Sometimes, we face overlapping challenges. Despite the
heavy burden of a particularly difficult situation, there may be minor
issues that also need our attention. When the more serious issue requires all of our attention, it must be prioritized. The minor issues can
wait for later. However, sometimes the larger issue can't be dealt with
or solved immediately. Rather than succumbing to feelings of being

overwhelmed, it is important to take care of the other minor issues that are in our more direct and immediate control.

Along similar lines, we sometimes have important goals that are not attainable in the present. Constant focus on those goals can prevent us from accomplishing smaller goals in the present. Richard Carlson writes:

> *Sometimes our grandiose plans to do great things at some later time interfere with our chances to do little things right now. A friend once told me, "I want my life to be about service, but I can't do anything yet. Someday, when I'm really successful, I'll do lots of things for others." Meanwhile, there are hungry people in the streets, elderly people who could use some company, mothers who need help with their children, people who can't read, neighbors whose homes need paint, streets with litter, people who need to be listened to, and thousands and thousands of other little things that need to be done.[1]*

Focus on what you can accomplish now.

---

[1]   *Don't Sweat the Small Stuff*, p. 201.

22a

COMPASSION

הלא כה דברי כאש נאם ה', מה אש אינו מקבל
טומאה אף דברי תורה אינן מקבלין טומאה.

"My word is like fire, says Hashem." Just as fire can
never become impure, so too words of Torah can never
become impure.

The Torah is compared to fire. One of the properties of fire is its
ability to cook, which the *Mishnah Berurah* explains, in the name of
the *Rambam*, is defined as softening a hard substance.[1] The Gemara in
Beitzah quotes Rabbi Meir, who says that the Torah was given to the
Jewish People because they are tough.[2] *Rashi* explains that the Torah
was given to us in order to humble us so that our toughness should not
go untamed. The Torah, which is a fire, softens us.

Gedolei Torah throughout the generations have possessed beautiful
soft-hearted personalities. The following story is from *The Palace
on 5 Chazon Ish Street*, a collection of stories about Rav Aharon Leib
Steinman.[3]

---

1   *Mishnah Berurah* 318:1.
2   *Beitzah* 25b.
3   *The Palace on 5 Chazon Ish Street*, p. 74.

One day, a mouse found its way into the little house on 5 Chazon Ish...As mice are wont to do, this first mouse brought a few friends after him, and these invaders became increasingly bold. Seeking to eliminate them, the family members looked around and pinpointed the spot where the mice were coming from...Rav Shteinman's confidant and right-hand man, Rav Shub, put out a trap, and the next day, a mouse was caught...This mouse didn't know how lucky he was to have been caught in precisely this place, the home of Rav Shteinman. In this house, its fate would be different from those of other trapped rodents. "Don't kill it," Rav Shteinman instructed. "Please take the trap and free the mouse far from where people live, so that it can continue to live without harming anyone." The devoted confidant...took a trip to the fields outside B'nei Brak. As they were walking, they received a call from Rav Shteinman's house. "The Rav wants to know if the mouse was freed. It's almost time for the Rav's afternoon shiur, and he is very perturbed over the suffering of the mouse, so it is difficult for him to go give the shiur.

When we learn Torah, it softens us. It enhances our consideration for others and it makes us more compassionate people.

The Torah makes us compassionate people who are sensitive to others.

22a

VALUE DAILY DECISIONS BUT HAVE A BROADER SELF-CONCEPT

מעשה באחד שתבע אשה לדבר עבירה. אמרה
לו: ריקא! יש לך ארבעים סאה שאתה טובל בהן?
מיד פירש.

A man tried to seduce a woman to sin. She said to him, "Empty one [i.e., fool], do you have forty *se'ah* [i.e., a kosher mikvah] in which to purify yourself so that you will be able to study Torah [as Ezra enacted]?" He immediately desisted.

Isn't it surprising that a person willing to violate a serious prohibition (notwithstanding the fact that *Rashi* interprets the Gemara as referring to an unmarried woman) would be deterred by the realization that he will then be prevented from learning Torah?

The Mishnah in *Gittin* teaches that before a widow collects her *kesubah*, she must take an oath that she has not already received her payment. When Chazal saw that widows were swearing falsely with the rationalization that they are entitled to extra payment in exchange for all of the work they do in caring for the orphaned children, they discontinued the practice of allowing the widow to take an oath. The result was that the widows were now unable to collect their *kesubah*. Rabban Gamliel devised a solution to this problem. The widow would take a vow that if she has already received her *kesubah*, she will no longer continue eating a staple food, e.g., grain products, for the rest of her life.[1]

What did this *takanah* of Rabban Gamliel accomplish?

The *Yerushalmi*, quoted by the *Tosafos Yom Tov*, explains that even though oaths are more severe than vows, the women were more fearful of violating a vow than an oath and were not suspect of rationalizing and being untruthful (as we sometimes find that the community relates to a particular minor prohibition with greater severity than a prohibition which in truth is more severe).

Tosafos explains that even if a woman would rationalize and lie, it would not be as bad because a vow is not as severe as an oath.[2]

The *Rosh* provides a third explanation. He begins by asking why it is that we don't bring a loaf of bread to the court and have the widow take a vow that if she received her *kesubah* already, she won't eat from it. We could then insist that she eat the bread. The *Rosh* answers that she would be willing to violate her vow and eat the bread because it is a one-time violation. She would also willingly violate the one-time prohibition of taking a false oath. We can only trust that she would not create a lifelong prohibition for herself because she would not want to continuously violate her vow for her entire life.[3]

From both our Gemara in *Berachos*, and this Mishnah in *Gittin*, we learn that it is human nature to be prepared to do something wrong in the moment, even if it is a severe prohibition, whereas to be very hesitant about creating a situation where one will constantly be in violation of minor prohibitions. What is the reason for this?

Perhaps it is because our self-concept of who we are is based on our long-term conduct. If we do something wrong in the moment, even if it is intentional, we tell ourselves, "That's not who I am." If we were to

---

1   Mishnah, *Gittin* 4:3.

2   *Gittin* 35a.

3   Mishnah, *Gittin* 4:8.

"commit" to doing something wrong on a regular basis, we would be forced to look ourselves in the mirror and admit, "That is who I am." On the one hand, this perspective is healthy. If we judged ourselves critically for every mistake that we made it would decrease our self-esteem and cripple us. It is more reasonable and more adaptive to view ourselves as a totality, looking at everything that we do, the good and the bad, over a considerable amount of time. Sometimes we have a bad day, and that doesn't define who we are. On the other hand, there is also a downside to this perspective. It overlooks the fact that who we are is created by every action and every decision. If we tell ourselves, "Now I'll do this, but from now on I'll be the person I want to be," we will find that we use this rationalization too frequently. Every action builds on preceding ones, and mistakes can affect us and lead us in the wrong direction.

The Mishnah in *Pirkei Avos* teaches that a mitzvah leads to another mitzvah, whereas a sin leads to another sin.[4] The Gemara in *Kiddushin* teaches that once a person violates a sin twice his perspective toward the sin changes and he begins to take it more lightly, as if it were actually something which is permitted.[5]

John Maxwell writes:

> The secret of your success is determined by your daily agenda. If you make a few key decisions and then manage them well in your daily agenda, you will succeed...The way you live your life today is preparing you for tomorrow...There are two ingredients necessary to make every day a masterpiece: decisions and discipline...It seems obvious that good decisions help to create a better tomorrow, yet many people don't appear to connect their lack of success to their poor decision-making...Others know their choices may not be good for them, but they make

---

4   *Avos* 4:2.
5   *Kiddushin* 20a.

them anyway...Nobody says that good decisions are always simple, but they are necessary for success.[6]

Define your self-concept broadly, not based on one action or one mistake. And recognize that every action contributes to making you who you will ultimately be in the long term.

---

6   *Make Today Count*, introduction.

22b

CREATIVITY

ירד לטבול, אם יכול לעלות ולהתכסות ולקרות עד
שלא תהא הנץ החמה—יעלה ויתכסה ויקרא, ואם
לאו—יתכסה במים ויקרא.

One who entered the mikvah to purify himself, if he
is able [i.e., has time] to emerge, dress, and recite the
Shema before sunrise, he should do so. If not, he should
clothe himself in the water and recite the *Shema*.

"**Functional** fixedness is the tendency to perceive an object only in terms of its most common use."[1] It takes creativity to notice that an object can be used for an entirely different purpose.

Normally, the waters of the mikvah are intended to purify. Chazal noticed that the waters of the mikvah can also be used to clothe a person who is otherwise undressed to enable them to recite *Shema*.

Imagine a person in the mikvah who notices that he does not have sufficient time to emerge and get dressed before the deadline for reciting *Shema*. He feels pressured, overwhelmed, and stuck. He has a real problem with no solution. He starts to panic. From our Mishnah, we

---

1   APA Dictionary.

can learn that in situations like this, it is important to think out of the box and to get creative.

John Maxwell presents a list of questions that a person can ask themselves to stimulate creativity: "Why must it be done this way? What is the root problem? What are the underlying issues? What does this remind me of? What is the opposite? What metaphor or symbol helps to explain it? Why is it important? What's the hardest or most expensive way to do it? Who has a different perspective on this? What happens if we don't do it at all?"[2]

What does it take to be creative? Must we think up the impossible? Maxwell quotes Sam Weston with the following observation:

> *"Truly groundbreaking ideas are rare, but you don't necessarily need one to make a career out of creativity. My definition of creativity is the logical combination of two or more existing elements that result in a new concept. The best way to make a living with your imagination is to develop innovative applications, not imagine completely new concepts."*[3]

Maxwell adds his own additional comment to foster creativity: "Most limitations we face are not imposed on us by others; we place them on ourselves. Lack of creativity often falls into this category."

Be creative. Think out of the box. Ask yourself questions that foster creativity. Think about existing ideas that can be combined in new productive ways.

---

2   *How Successful People Think*, p. 32.
3   Ibid., p. 34.

22b

SPEND TIME IN A PLEASANT AESTHETIC ENVIRONMENT

היה עומד בתפלה וראה צואה כנגדו—מהלך לפניו
עד שיזרקנה לאחוריו ארבע אמות.

If a person is davening and notices that the place in
which he is davening is dirty and unfit for prayer, he
should move forward so that the area that is unclean is
four *amos* behind him.

The place where a person davens must be clean. The Gemara on 24b
applies the *pasuk*, "For he has disgraced the word of Hashem,"[1] to one
who recites *Shema* in a place that is unclean. To show proper respect
for an activity, it must be done in a clean and respectable place. This is
especially true when the activity is one of great spiritual significance
such as davening.

While of course this is true of a shul and a *beis midrash*, it is also true of
the place where we live and work. Spending time in a clean and respectable room sends us the message that what we are doing is important
and, by extension, that we are important.

---

1   *Bamidbar* 15:31.

Richard Carlson writes:

> *I wish I could include a photograph of my office in this book. It's bright, inviting, friendly looking, and peaceful. In fact, it's so happiness-oriented that it's almost impossible to get depressed while you're in it. Most people who visit fall in love with it and claim they almost always feel better when they leave. Yet I can assure you that my office is not fancy, and is certainly not expensively decorated...You spend an enormous amount of time where you work. Why not take a tiny bit of time, energy, and money and brighten it up, even a little?...Try a few pictures, a brighter rug, inspirational books, freshly cut flowers, goldfish, signs of nature, or some combination. You'd be amazed at what a drawing from a child can do to lift your spirits...It's really nice to walk in and feel good about where you are going to spend your day. Make it bright, cheery and friendly, and it's pretty hard to walk in and not feel the same way.*[2]

Take the places where you spend much of your time and turn them into aesthetically pleasing and friendly environments.

---

2   Richard Carlson, *Don't Sweat the Small Stuff at Work*, p. 52.

23a

OBSESSIONS AND COMPULSIONS

הנצרך לנקביו—אל יתפלל.

One may not daven at a time when they feel the need to
relieve themselves.

One common manifestation of religious Obsessive-Compulsive
Disorder (OCD) is the obsession over bathroom cleanliness before davening. With regard to the particular discussion on our *daf*, the *Kuntres
Yirah Tehorah* quotes *poskim* who write that if one would not feel that
they had to relieve themselves if they were distracted by an activity,
they may daven. Beyond this particular application, though, it is important to understand the concept behind OCD and how it is treated.

When a person suffers from OCD, they have an intrusive thought that
they believe may be potentially dangerous. They also frequently believe
that if they don't neutralize the thought, they will be plagued by anxiety
and fear of the danger that they associate with the thought. For example, one who has the intrusive thought that they are contaminated
may not only fear the effects of contamination (germs, becoming ill,
etc.), but may also fear that they will not be able to tolerate the anxiety
that they are currently feeling. This leads to neutralizing behaviors
such as excessive washing. When the catastrophe they feared does not
come true (they don't become ill), they attribute it to the neutralizing

behaviors and rituals rather than to the fact that there was never a real danger.

Adrian Wells notes that several factors contribute to OCD. They are: perfectionistic beliefs, an inflated sense of responsibility, cognitive deficits in decision-making, thought-action fusion (believing that a thought of doing something terrible is equivalent to actually doing it, or believing that thinking about something will lead to it actually happening), and meta-cognitive beliefs (beliefs about intrusive thoughts, e.g., "I'll be plagued by anxiety if I don't neutralize the thought").[1]

The primary components of treatment are verbally challenging the above factors, especially the meta-cognitive beliefs about the intrusive thought, and exposure and response prevention.

With regard to addressing the meta-cognitive beliefs, Adrian Wells writes, "Negative appraisals concerning the unremitting nature of discomfort or worry should rituals/checking be abandoned should be challenged by questioning the evidence for this belief."[2]

In exposure and response prevention, the person is exposed to their fear (they touch something that probably has germs, such as opening a public door) and they refrain from their neutralizing ritual (they don't wash their hands afterward). Adrian Wells explains how this works. He writes:

> In a cognitive therapy framework, the rationale should emphasize exposure to thoughts, contaminants, or events as a means of challenging beliefs concerning the catastrophic nature of contact with such stimuli. Response prevention (or elimination of safety behaviors) then becomes a discomfirmitory maneuver that facilitates attribution of the non-occurrence of catastrophe to the falseness of the original belief.[3]

When it comes to religious expressions of OCD, using exposure and response prevention presents a challenge. The intrusive thought that

---

1   *Cognitive Therapy of Anxiety Disorders*, p. 237.
2   Ibid., p. 255.
3   Ibid., p. 258.

the person is concerned with is frequently that they have a particular religious obligation to do something. Someone who repeats *Shema* tens of times until they are satisfied that they have fulfilled their obligation believes that if they don't repeat *Shema* again, they will not have fulfilled their obligation. How can he listen to us when we tell him, "Don't say *Shema* again and you will see that there are no negative consequences"?

Rav Asher Weiss permits exposure and response prevention based on the following ideas:

1. A person is not required to give up more than a fifth of their possessions in order to fulfill a positive commandment. Since a person's mental health is worth much more than a fifth of their possessions, a person doesn't need to sacrifice their mental health in order to fulfill a positive commandment. Even if the person is correct that without repeating *Shema* they will not have fulfilled the mitzvah, if that is what is necessary to restore their mental health, it is permitted.

2. Even the violation of a negative commandment can be permitted; this is based on an idea similar to the halachah that one may violate Shabbos to save a life because it is better to violate one Shabbos now so that the person will be able to keep many Shabbosos in the future. So too, violating one prohibition now in order to restore the person's mental health will facilitate the performance of many mitzvos in the future.[4] (This second concept has halachically relevant nuances. See Rav Asher Weiss's *teshuvah* inside or speak to a Rav before practically applying this concept.)

Combat OCD by cognitively challenging the factors that contribute to OCD, and through exposure and response prevention.

---

4   *Shu"t Minchas Asher*, vol. 2, 134.

23a

HOPELESSNESS

ומעשה בתלמיד אחד שהניח תפיליו בחורין
הסמוכים לרשות הרבים, ובאת זונה אחת ונטלתן,
ובאת לבית המדרש ואמרה: ראו מה נתן לי פלוני
בשכרי! כיון ששמע אותו תלמיד כך, עלה לראש
הגג ונפל ומת.

A certain Torah student once left his tefillin in a hole in
the fence next to the public street. A harlot took them
and came to the *beis midrash*. She said, "Look what so-
and-so gave me as my hire!" When the student heard
this, he went up to the roof, jumped down, and died.

What leads a person to contemplate taking their own life?

Because of the severity of this question, let's look at some highlights
from a chapter on suicide that was written by one of the world's leading
experts of Cognitive Behavioral Therapy.

Dr. David Burns writes:

*When you feel down in the dumps, you may also feel so low
at times that you get the feeling you were never really happy
and never will be. If a friend or relative points out to you that,*

except for such periods of depression, you were quite happy, you may conclude they're mistaken or only trying to cheer you up. This is because while you are depressed you actually distort your memories of the past. You just can't conjure up any memories of periods of satisfaction or joy, so you erroneously conclude that you always have been and always will be miserable...No matter how bad you feel, it would be bearable if you had the conviction that things would eventually improve. The critical decision to commit suicide results from your illogical conviction that your mood can't improve. You feel certain that the future holds only more pain and turmoil...Research studies have shown that your unrealistic sense of hopelessness is one of the most crucial factors in the development of a serious suicidal wish...When you are depressed, you may have a tendency to confuse feelings with facts. Your feelings of hopelessness and total despair are just symptoms of depressive illness, not facts. If you think you are hopeless, you will naturally feel this way. Your feelings only trace the illogical pattern of your thinking. Only an expert, who has treated hundreds of depressed individuals, would be in a position to give a meaningful prognosis for recovery. Your suicidal urge merely indicates the need for treatment. Thus, your conviction that you are "hopeless" nearly always proves you are not. Therapy, not suicide, is indicated. Although generalizations can be misleading, I let the following rule of thumb guide me: Patients who feel hopelessness never actually are hopeless...You may feel that you are caught in a trap from which there is no exit. This may lead to extreme frustration and even to the urge to kill yourself as the only escape. However, when I confront a depressed patient with respect to precisely what kind of trap he or she is in, and I zero in on the person's "insoluble problem," I invariably find that the patient is deluded...Your suicidal thoughts are illogical, distorted, and erroneous. Your twisted thoughts and faulty assumptions, not reality, create your suffering. When you learn to look behind

the mirrors, you will see that you are fooling yourself, and your
suicidal urge will disappear.[1]

The Gemara in *Avodah Zarah* relates that after Adam HaRishon sinned, he noticed that as fall progressed toward winter, the days began to get shorter and shorter. Not knowing that this was the natural transition of the seasons (as this was the first year of creation), he feared that he was heading toward the death that G-d had decreed upon him as punishment for his sin of eating from the Tree of Knowledge.[2] Indeed, G-d had warned him of his punishment and the world was becoming enveloped in darkness. What more evidence could he need. Surely, the situation was helpless. His future held only darkness and destruction. After several months, the spring arrived. Now the days grew gradually longer as the sun shone its friendly warmth on Adam and the world. Adam realized that such was the natural way of the world. There are seasons of darkness that give way to seasons of light.

Sometimes there are situations that appear very dark. There may even be "evidence" that seems to indicate that nothing will ever change. However, if we look carefully at this "evidence," we will see that it is faulty. Ultimately, situations change, problems are resolved, and challenges are overcome.

The *Yerushalmi* at the beginning of *Berachos* tells us that once, Rabbi Chiya was going for a walk very early in the morning. When the dawn rose, he exclaimed, "Such shall be the redemption of the Jewish People. At the beginning it will be gradual and it will continue to grow (just as the dawn begins with a sliver of light and continues until the powerful midday sun)." Rabbi Chiya quoted the *pasuk* in *Michah*, "As I sit in darkness, Hashem is my light,"[3] and applied it to the Purim story.[4] The redemption was slow and gradual. It began with Mordechai sitting at the gates of the palace. Later, he was honored by Achashverosh, as Haman was ordered to parade him through Shushan riding on the king's horse.

---

1   *Feeling Good*, p. 384.
2   *Avodah Zarah* 8a.
3   *Michah* 7:8.
4   *Yerushalmi, Berachos* 1:1.

After the parade, he returned to the gates of the palace. Eventually, the *pasuk* tells us that he emerged from before the king dressed in royal garments, and finally that the Jewish People had joy, light, and honor.

Just as the collective redemption of the Jewish People is a process that develops gradually, so too with individuals who feel enveloped in darkness. There are improvements and setbacks—two steps forward and one step back—until the situation improves. After Mordechai was honored with the royal parade, he returned to where he had previously been at the gates of the palace. He had taken two steps forward and one step back. Shortly after, he continued with forward progress. With persistence, patience, and time, the suffering will dissipate, and joy will return.

When one is suffering, it is sometimes difficult to see how anything could improve. One sees "evidence" to support that prediction of hopelessness. It is important to challenge the "evidence" and recognize its fallacies. Be aware that the emotional state one is in can have an effect on the interpretation of the evidence that one sees and on the counter-evidence that one doesn't notice. With persistence and patience, even the darkest situations will improve.

23b

MINDFULNESS AND FOCUS

לא יאחז אדם תפילין בידו וספר תורה בזרועו
ויתפלל...אמר שמואל: סכין, ומעות, וקערה, וככר
הרי אלו כיוצא בהן.

One should not hold tefillin or a *Sefer Torah* in one's
hands while davening...So too, one should not hold a knife,
money, a bowl, or a loaf of bread. [*Rashi* explains that the
concern that any of these items will fall will distract the
person from focusing on their davening.]

Distractions detract from our ability to accomplish. If we
try to do too many things at the same time, we will not be able to do our
best at any of them.

In *Sifsei Chaim*, Rav Friendlander defines "peace of mind" as when "a
person lives with the internalized feeling, and not only the intellectual
recognition, to use every moment with full concentration of thought
and effort, for only the task at hand. A person can't do many things
at the same time. Even a person who has many different skills uses

the appropriate skill for what he is currently doing, and doesn't mix in thoughts about the past and future into his current activity."[1]

In Dialectical Behavioral Therapy (DBT), this skill is known as "one-mindfully." Mazza et al write:

> *Experiments have been completed where people were given a list of tasks to complete as quickly as possible. The results showed that people who completed the tasks one at a time, as opposed to multitasking, had greater levels of accuracy and completed the tasks faster...One-mindfully means doing only one thing at a time, in the moment, with awareness and alertness. Focusing attention on only one thing helps bring the whole person to the activity...Texting while driving is not driving one-mindfully. It is doing more than one thing at a time. It can cause fatal accidents...When we practice our mindfulness exercises, we practice doing one thing in the moment.[2]*

Devote yourself to one thing at a time, and you will greatly increase your peace of mind.

---

1   *Sifsei Chaim, Middos V'Avodas Hashem*, vol. 2, p. 17.
2   Mazza et al, *DBT Skills in Schools*, p. 99.

24a

FIND POINTS OF AGREEMENT

אמר לך שמואל: לרב יוסף מי ניחא?...אלא מאי
אית לך למימר—אשתו לרב יוסף תנאי היא, לדידי
נמי תנאי היא.

[Shmuel and Rav Yosef differed with regard to a particular halachah. The Gemara tells us that] Shmuel would
reply to Rav Yosef by saying the following: "Even Rav
Yosef's explanation will not suffice...He must concede
that his position is a matter of dispute. So too, I will also
maintain that my position is a matter of dispute [and
though you have proven that some disagree with my
position, I will maintain that others agree with me."]

Shmuel's method of debate here is to note that Rav Yosef's position is not uniformly accepted in its entirety. One aspect of his position,
even he must concede, is a matter of dispute amongst the Tanna'im.
Shmuel then acknowledges that his own position is also not uniformly
accepted. He is in effect noting that the difference between his position
and that of Rav Yosef's is not about whether either of their positions
are legitimate or illegitimate. Both of their positions are tannaitic. The
only debate is with regard to how to *pasken* the halachah.

Sometimes, it is helpful in a disagreement to point out to the other person that you agree with their position in certain cases, and that even they will presumably agree that their position is not uniform, and that in some remote cases they would agree with your position. It is then possible to explain the difference of opinion in terms of degrees rather than in terms of fundamentals. So long as the other person believes that your position is diametrically opposed to his, he will be less open to hearing out your point of view. If he recognizes that you agree on the fundamentals and disagree on the application in a specific case, it will be easier to have a mutually understanding dialogue.

The same idea can be applied to difficult interpersonal situations. By acknowledging and implying that there is some truth to the other person's complaint, and that you are interested in hearing more about it, you convey to them that you really want to listen and hear them out. It is then safe to imply gently that even they would agree that the issue may not be as bad as they are making it out to be.

Dr. Mark Goulston explains this idea in his book, *Just Listen*. He writes:

> *When a person launches into an out-of-control rant about how awful the problem is and how it's the end of the world, etc. Scott simply says, calmly: "Do you really believe that?" This is a highly effective question, because when you ask it in a calm way, it causes most people who use hyperbole or exaggeration to recant and restate their position. Typically, they backpedal by saying something like, "Well, not really, but I am very frustrated about things." Then you can respond, "I understand that, but I need to know what the truth is, because if what you say is totally true, then we have a serious problem and need to address it."…The trick to this approach is to ask the question ("Do you really believe that?") not in a hostile or degrading manner, but very calmly and in a straightforward way.*[1]

---

1   Dr. Mark Goulston, *Just Listen*, p. 138.

What Dr. Goulston's question essentially does is it acknowledges that the other person's complaint is to some degree valid. If you didn't believe that it was valid at all, you wouldn't inquire about it at all. At the same time, it asks the other person to acknowledge that it isn't really as bad as they are presenting it. It is then possible to discuss the issue mutually and productively.

Acknowledge that there is truth to the other person's perspective. Ask if they believe that there is an aspect of truth to your perspective. After you both understand each other, find the point of dispute to discuss productively.

24b

CONVEYING PREFERENCES

המשמיע קולו בתפלתו הרי זה מקטני אמנה. אמר
רב הונא: לא שנו אלא שיכול לכוין את לבו בלחש,
אבל אין יכול לכוין את לבו בלחש—מותר; והני
מילי—ביחיד, אבל בצבור—אתי למיטרד צבורא.

One who davens *Shemoneh Esreh* out loud is of little
faith. Says Rav Huna: "This is only if he is able to concentrate while davening quietly. If not, he is permitted
to daven out loud. However, this is only if he is davening
alone. If he is davening with the congregation, he must
daven quietly so as not to disturb the congregation."

Davening *Shemoneh Esreh* loudly is inappropriate because it implies that Hashem can't hear a silent *tefillah*. Nonetheless, if one can't
concentrate when davening quietly, one may daven out loud, provided
that he is davening privately. If he is davening with the congregation,
however, there is a concern that if he davens out loud it will be hard for
the other congregants to concentrate.

The Gemara in several places uses the phrase, "We do not derive a case where it is possible, from a case where it is impossible."[1] One application of this law is as follows: There is an opinion that vessels used in the Beis Hamikdash must be constructed from metal. This is despite the fact that we know that the flute used in the Bais Hamikdash to accompany the singing of *Hallel* was made of wood and not metal. It was made during the lifetime of Moshe Rabbeinu and presumably with his guidance. Wouldn't this indicate that vessels in the Beis Hamikdash may be constructed from wood as well? The Gemara explains that a metal flute would not produce a proper sound, and therefore it was necessary to make the flute from wood. We do not derive from here that other vessels may be made from wood because other vessels could accomplish their function just as well, even if they were made of metal. In other words, "We do not derive a case where it is possible [to do differently] from a case where it is impossible [to do differently, and this is the only possible option]."

This is an important principle to apply in everyday life. We sometimes have preferences about certain things. When they can be accommodated, that is wonderful. When they are not possible, that is also OK. When asking someone to do something for us, we may want to convey to them that we have a preference, but we don't want to cause them stress by making them think that if it doesn't work out, we will be upset. We don't want to say that it doesn't matter to us, because it truly does matter, and we want the other person to take the request seriously. We just don't want them to stress about it. The ideal way to convey this type of request is by explaining to them that we would really appreciate it if it is possible, and we will be very understanding if it is not possible.

Look at each case independently. Is it necessary in this case?
Is it practical or possible in this case? Make polite requests
to accommodate your preferences, and be sensitive to avoid
causing stress when the fulfillment of requests isn't possible.

---

1   *Sukkah* 50b.

24b

ASCRIBE POSITIVE MOTIVATIONS

אמר רב יהודה: כל העולה מבבל לארץ ישראל עובר
בעשה, שנאמר: בבלה יובאו ושמה יהיו עד יום פקדי
אותם נאם ה'.

Rav Yehudah says: Anyone who moves from Bavel to
Eretz Yisrael is in violation of a positive commandment,
as it says, "You will be brought to Bavel, and there you
will remain until the day when I redeem you, the word of
Hashem."

Do we ever question other people's motives? If we do, we may be
engaging in the cognitive distortion of mind-reading. The Gemara
in *Pesachim* tells us that we can never know what is in our friend's
heart.[1] We may guess what someone else is thinking, but we can never
know for sure.

Rav Yehudah was of the belief that it is forbidden to return to Eretz
Yisrael before the coming of Mashiach. Why did he say that? What were
his motives? Perhaps one might mistakenly think that he lacked a true
love for Eretz Yisrael.

---

1   *Pesachim* 54b.

The Gemara on *daf* 43a asks, "What *berachah* is recited before smelling *Afarsimon* oil?" Rav Yehuda replied *"Baruch Atah Hashem...* Who created the oil of our land." The Gemara rejects this and says "We can't accept Rav Yehudah's answer because he has great love for Eretz Yisrael. What do others say the *berachah* should be?"

Rav Yehudah is not only not guilty of lacking love for Eretz Yisrael, but is in fact the Amora who was known for being the one to have the greatest love for Eretz Yisrael! His opinion forbidding the return to Eretz Yisrael before the coming of Mashiach was therefore not due to improper motives. It was due to his pure understanding of the *pasuk* that he quotes in his derivation of this halachah. While we may disagree with another's viewpoint, we should not be so arrogant as to be certain what their motivation or thought process is. Perhaps they excel in the very trait that we think they are lacking. Perhaps the insensitivities that we attribute to them are not true. Perhaps they are on an even higher level than we are in the very same area where we call them into question.

We can never know the motivation behind the actions, words, or viewpoints of another person. While you may disagree with their viewpoint, judge their motivation favorably.

24b

DO MORE GOOD THAN HARM

היה מהלך במבואות המטונפות—לא יקרא קריאת
שמע; ולא עוד אלא שאם היה קורא ובא—פוסק.
לא פסק מאי...רב אסי אמר: הוי מושכי העון
בחבלי השוא.

If one is walking through a dirty alleyway, he may not
recite *Shema*. Even if he was in the middle of reciting
Shema, he must stop. If he does not stop, he is in
violation of the *pasuk*, "Woe to those who pull sin upon
themselves with cords of nothingness."

Why does the Gemara apply this *pasuk* to one who recites *Shema* in
a dirty alleyway in which it is forbidden to do so?

Rashi explains that "cords of nothingness" refers to the fact that they
are sinning through mere words that lack tangible substance. *Tosafos*
explains that they are sinning for no reason, and that it would be preferable if they wouldn't have uttered anything at all.

The explanation of *Tosafos* is reminiscent of the concept of "*mishkal
ha'chassidus.*" When performing a mitzvah it is important to assess
whether we may be causing harm in other ways. In certain cases, it may

not be worth it to perform the mitzvah if the way in which it is done causes more harm than good.

Rav Pam illustrated this idea with the following example:

> *It is a great mitzvah to gladden a chassan and kallah, but I do not approve of that which I have often seen—that young, married b'nei Torah dance at weddings until late into the night, without consideration of their parents who are sitting back home bleary-eyed as they babysit for their grandchildren. Even if a girl had been hired to babysit, it is not proper to delay returning home until a very late hour, for many reasons. To perform acts of chessed is a great mitzvah and a good middah, but not when it is at someone else's expense. All the more so if that "someone else" is one's wife! For example: A husband usually arrives home for supper at 6:00 pm after a day in the beis midrash or at work. His wife has prepared a sumptuous meal in accordance with his tastes, and she is awaiting his arrival. The clock ticks on...6:05...6:15...6:30...he has not come home. More time passes, and now the wife is quite worried. What has happened? And what should she do with the food so that it will not burn or lose its freshness? Suddenly, the door opens, and in walks her husband. He has an excuse: his friend needed to catch a plane, so he graciously drove him to the airport. How sad that he did not consider his wife's distress; at the very least, this would have impelled him to contact her and gain her approval.[1]*

This last example is very similar to a frightening Gemara in *Masechta Kesubos*. "Rav Rechumei was a student of Rava in the town of Mechuza. Every year, he would return home on Erev Yom Kippur. One year, he was drawn into his learning and he didn't come home. His wife gazed with anticipation, eagerly awaiting his arrival, and telling herself, 'He will come soon, he will come soon.' He did not come. She felt terrible and a tear fell from her eyes. At that moment Rav Rechumei was sitting

---

1   *The Life and Ideals of Rav Avraham Yaakov HaKohen Pam*, p. 179.

on the roof. The roof fell from beneath him and he passed away."[2] This sad and powerful story is a reminder to never allow ourselves to do what may appear to be good, but in reality is a serious sin, because it is hurtful to others.

If this is true when it comes to valuable mitzvos such as engrossment in Torah study and bringing joy to a *chassan* and *kallah*, then certainly it is true about professional ambitions or other pursuits. Whenever we make a decision that affects others, we have to weigh the pros and cons and take into account the effect that our decision will have on other people. If we are causing them more harm than the good we bring about through the action, it just isn't worth it.

Consider the possible side effects of the mitzvah, or any activity that you are planning to do. Ensure that the good that you hope to do will not be at the expense of causing greater harm.

---

2   *Kesubos* 62b.

25a

REVIEW TO INTERNALIZE

אבל לתפלה—עד שיכסה את לבו.
To daven *Shemoneh Esreh*, one must be fully clothed
[lit., "cover his heart"].

In order to daven *Shemoneh Esreh*, one must be fully clothed. *Rashi* explains that davening is standing before the King. He adds, "It is not similar to reciting *Shema* [which does not require being completely clothed,] because when we recite *Shema*, we are not considered to be standing before the King."

Since *Shema* is such an integral part of davening, it can be confused for a "prayer." In fact, *Shema* is not a prayer. It is a reminder that we give ourselves consistently of some of the most important fundamentals of Judaism.

The *Mesilas Yesharim* begins his introduction as follows:

> *I have written this work not to teach people what they do not know, but rather to remind them of what they already know and clearly understand...However, to the degree that these rules are well-known and their truth self-evident, they are routinely overlooked, or people forget about them altogether. Therefore, the benefit to be obtained from this work cannot*

be derived from a single reading; for it is possible that, after just one reading, the reader will find that he had learned little that he did not know before. Rather, its benefit is a function of continuous review. In this manner, one is reminded of those things that, by nature, people are prone to forget, and he will take to heart the duty that he tends to overlook.[1]

In order to internalize important truths, it is necessary to review them constantly. This is true both with regard to fundamentals of *Yahadus*, as well as any concept that could contribute to a person's personal growth. Judith Beck writes,

Having evaluated an automatic thought with patients, you will then ask them to summarize. When patients express a cogent summary, you can ask them if they would like to record it, so they can better remember the response when similar automatic thoughts arise in the future...It is desirable to have patients read their therapy notes each morning and pull them out, as needed, during the day. Patients tend to integrate responses into their thinking when they have rehearsed them repeatedly. Reading notes only when encountering difficult situations is usually less effective than reading them regularly in preparation for difficult situations.[2]

Take the ideas that you want to internalize and repeat them consistently. Through constant review they will become a part of you.

---

1   *Mesilas Yesharim*, Feldheim translation.
2   *CBT Basics and Beyond*, p. 188.

25b

THE PLEASANTNESS
AND DELIGHT OF TORAH

לא נתנה תורה למלאכי השרת.

The Torah was not given to the ministering angels.

Hakadosh Baruch Hu gave us a Torah that requires effort to fulfill, but is not intended to be excessively challenging. If a particular halachah would be too difficult to fulfill, it would not be required. The Torah was not given to the ministering angels who are on levels of perfection that we, as humans, cannot attain.

The Gemara in *Shabbos* quotes a Mishnah that teaches that if one lights his Chanukah menorah outside and a camel laden with flax catches fire, the lighter of the menorah is exempt from paying damages because he has permission to light the Chanukah menorah outside. The Gemara derives from here that, seemingly, the menorah should be placed ideally within ten *tefachim* of the ground. If this were not so, there would be an obligation to light the menorah higher up so as to avoid causing potential damage. The Gemara rejects this proof by suggesting that perhaps the menorah may be lit above ten *tefachim*, however we don't insist that people do this. If we would trouble them to such an extent, they would refrain from fulfilling the mitzvah of lighting the menorah at all.[1]

The Torah refers to the lulav as a *"kapos temarim."*[2] We know that *"temarim"* are dates and that the lulav must come from a palm tree. When the Gemara in *Sukkah* is seeking to identify which part of the palm tree is called a *kapos temarim*, the Gemara suggests that perhaps it is a branch that grew recently and has sharp thorn-like protrusions. The Gemara rejects this suggestion based on the *pasuk*, "Its ways are ways of pleasantness, and all its pathways are peaceful."[3] Hashem would not command us to take a lulav that would injure our hands.

The Mishnah in *Gittin* presents a list of policies that are for the sake of "peace." The first policy mentioned is that a Kohen always receives the first *aliyah* to the Torah in order to prevent arguments that might arise over who will receive the first honor. The Gemara quotes a *Beraisa* that derives this policy from the word in the Torah *"v'kidashto,"* which teaches us to bestow the honor of going first in matters of holiness upon the Kohen. The Gemara then asks, "Why does our Mishnah say that this policy is for the sake of peace when it is in fact a Torah requirement to honor the Kohen?" The Gemara answers, "It is a Torah requirement for the sake of peace." The Gemara then asks, "All of the halachos of the Torah are for the sake of peace, as it says, 'Its ways are ways of pleasantness, and all its ways are peaceful.' Why then does the Mishnah single out these policies as being instituted for the sake of peace?" The Gemara goes on to answer its question, but the takeaway lesson for us here is that all of the halachos of the Torah were intended to be pleasant and peaceful.[4]

In *Parashas Nitzavim*, the Torah tells us, "[The Torah] is not in the heavens, for it is very close to you, in your mouths and in your hearts, to do it."[5] *Rashi* comments that the Written Torah was given

---

1   *Shabbos* 21b.
2   *Vayikra* 23:40.
3   *Sukkah* 32a.
4   *Gittin* 59a.
5   *Devarim* 30:13–14.

to us together with the Oral Torah. What is *Rashi* teaching us with this comment?

The *Sifsei Chachamim* explains that when one approaches learning, he may feel discouraged. Even though the Torah is not in heaven, it may still be very difficult to learn. The Torah is so deep and our understanding is so limited. *Rashi* therefore explains that we were given the Oral Torah to explain the Written Torah in a clear and easy-to-understand manner. The Torah really is very close to us. It is meant to be easy to understand and easy to learn. It isn't supposed to be a struggle. It's supposed to be a pleasure!

Where then is the place for toiling in learning?

The Mishnah in *Pirkei Avos* tells us, "Thus is the way of the Torah: eat bread with salt, drink water in small amounts, sleep on the ground, and toil in Torah."[6] *Rashi* explains that the Mishnah is not telling a rich person to forego the comforts he has accessible to him. Instead, it is telling a poor person that, despite his poverty, he still should engage in studying Torah. We also learn in *Pirkei Avos*, "Anyone who fulfills the Torah through poverty will ultimately fulfill it with wealth."[7] The ideal is to observe and learn Torah in comfort. Chazal tell us that learning requires a comfortable setting that is conducive to having clarity in one's learning.[8] Nevertheless, sometimes one finds himself in a situation where learning requires greater effort and overcoming difficulties. Even though that is not the ideal, one who loves Torah, and is committed to Torah, will try to overcome those obstacles to the best of his ability. That is *"ameilus baTorah,"* toiling in Torah.

David HaMelech sings about the Torah: "They are more desirable than gold or even much fine gold, and they are sweeter than honey." Hopefully, with Hashem's help, we will internalize the recognition that Torah is so sweet and precious, and we will merit the fulfillment of David HaMelech's *tefillah*: "One thing I asked from Hashem, that I will

---

6   *Avos* 6:4.
7   Ibid., 4:9.
8   *Megillah* 28b.

seek: That I would dwell in the House of Hashem all the days of my life, to see the sweetness of Hashem and to study[9] in His sanctuary."[10]

The Torah is pleasant, precious, and sweet!

---

9   See *Rashi, Metzudas David*, and *Ibn Ezra*.

10   *Tehillim* 27:4.

CONCLUSION

The *Mishnah Berurah* writes that one is obligated to set aside time daily for the study of *sifrei mussar* (books of personal growth).[1] There are many *sifrei mussar* available, both classics written by the great Rishonim, as well as contemporary *sefarim* of the great Acharonim. What form of preparation do we need before we approach the study of these powerful and inspirational works?

Rav Wolbe addresses a common problem that may arise as we begin our study of personal growth. He says,

> *Nobody is entirely free from the discomfort our conscience brings upon us for various misdeeds. When we begin to study growth, our conscience reminds us of our sins. Sadness dominates us and makes it difficult for us to see our importance and elevated status. We must overcome this so that our study of growth should not become barren. Let us learn of the preciousness of our souls. Only after we have internalized and truly experienced this realization of greatness may we begin to work on turning away from our shortcomings.[2]*

This *sefer*, *Psychology in the Talmud*, is the beginning of a process. Personal growth is a lifelong journey. Hopefully, the ideas of this *sefer*

---

1   *Mishnah Berurah* 1:12.
2   *Alei Shur*, vol. 1, p. 169, translated.

will enhance our happiness, our recognition of the greatness of man, our understanding of the process of growth, our ability to overcome setbacks, our ability to interact successfully with others, and our appreciation for Hashem and His Torah. With this positive frame of mind, we are ready to continue our journey of growth with joy and inspiration.

ABOUT THE AUTHOR

Rabbi Elihu Abbe had the *zechus* to learn full time for thirteen years, first as a *talmid* of Yeshivat Kerem B'Yavneh and then at RIETS (Yeshiva University), where he received *semichah*. He subsequently earned his MSW from Yeshiva University's Wurzweiler School of Social Work and certificates in Cognitive Behavioral Therapy, CBT for Depression, and CBT for Anxiety from the Beck Institute. He has taught Torah and *tikkun ha'middos* to *talmidim* of all ages as an elementary school social work intern, high school *bekius rebbi* and social work intern, *yeshiva gedolah shoel u'meishiv, sgan rosh beit midrash*, and shul rabbinic intern. He also enjoyed six summers working as a counselor at Morasha Kollel, organizing, caring for the *talmidim*, and offering guidance. Rabbi Abbe currently lives in Baltimore with his wife Eliana and his children, Rochel, Yosef, and Ephraim.

Rabbi Abbe can be reached at elihutuvia@gmail.com.

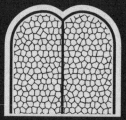

MOSAICA PRESS
BOOK PUBLISHERS

Elegant, Meaningful & Bold

info@MosaicaPress.com
www.MosaicaPress.com

The Mosaica Press team of
acclaimed editors and designers
is attracting some of the most
compelling thinkers and teachers
in the Jewish community today.
Our books are available around
the world.

HARAV YAACOV HABER
RABBI DORON KORNBLUTH